The World Guide to Sustainable Enterprise

Volume 2 – Asia Pacific

Other Books by Wayne Visser

Non-fiction

Sustainable Frontiers: Unlocking Change through Business, Leadership and Innovation

This is Tomorrow: Artists for a Sustainable Future (with A. Ardakani)

The CSR International Research Compendium: Volumes 1–3

Disrupting the Future: Great Ideas for Creating a Much Better World

CSR 2.0: Transforming Corporate Sustainability and Responsibility

The Quest for Sustainable Business: An Epic Journey in Search of Corporate Responsibility

Corporate Sustainability & Responsibility: An Introductory Text on CSR Theory & Practice – Past, Present & Future

The Age of Responsibility: CSR 2.0 and the New DNA of Business

The World Guide to CSR: A Country by Country Analysis of Corporate Sustainability and Responsibility (with N. Tolhurst)

The Top 50 Sustainability Books (with Cambridge Institute for Sustainability Leadership)

Landmarks for Sustainability: Events and Initiatives that Changed Our World (with Cambridge Institute for Sustainability Leadership)

Making A Difference: Purpose-Inspired Leadership for Corporate Sustainability & Responsibility

The A to Z of Corporate Social Responsibility: A Complete Reference Guide to Concepts, Codes and Organisations (with D. Matten, M. Pohl & N. Tolhurst)

Corporate Citizenship in Africa: Lessons from the Past, Paths to the Future (with M. McIntosh & C. Middleton)

Business Frontiers: Social Responsibility, Sustainable Development and Economic Justice

South Africa: Reasons to Believe (with G. Lundy)

Beyond Reasonable Greed: Why Sustainable Business is a Much Better Idea (with C. Sunter)

Fiction

Life in Transit: Favourite Travel & Tribute Poems

I Am An African: Favourite Africa Poems

Icarus: Favourite Love Poems

African Dream: Inspiring Words & Images from the Luminous Continent

String, Donuts, Bubbles and Me: Favourite Philosophical Poems

Seize the Day: Favourite Inspirational Poems

Wishing Leaves: Favourite Nature Poems

The World Guide
to Sustainable Enterprise

Volume 2: ASIA PACIFIC

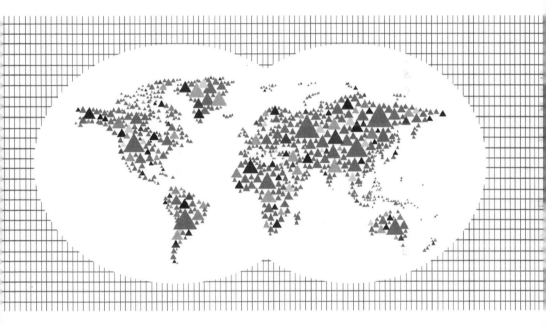

Wayne Visser

Routledge
Taylor & Francis Group

LONDON AND NEW YORK

First published 2016 by Greenleaf Publishing Limited

Published 2017 by Routledge
2 Park Square, Milton Park, Abingdon, Oxon OX14 4RN
711 Third Avenue, New York, NY 10017, USA

Routledge is an imprint of the Taylor & Francis Group, an informa business

Copyright © 2016 Taylor & Francis

Cover by Sadie Gornall-Jones

British Library Cataloguing in Publication Data:
    A catalogue record for this book is available from the British Library.

        ISBN-13: 978-1-78353-462-3 [hbk]
        ISBN-13: 978-1-78353-464-7 [pbk]

Contents

Introduction

When I published *The World Guide to CSR* in 2010, it was the most ambitious project of its kind, providing the most comprehensive country-by-country analysis of corporate sustainability and responsibility, with over 100 contributors profiling five regions and 58 countries. It remains an excellent reference book and I highly recommend it.

However, I am acutely aware of how fast the ideas and practices around social responsibility and sustainable business are evolving around the world, many of which I have observed at first hand in my work in over 70 countries, including more than 30 countries in the past five years. So I knew *The World Guide to CSR* needed updating, but I also knew the agenda had shifted.

One of the shifts I have become aware of is a move away from narrow conceptions of corporate social responsibility to a more multifaceted understanding. Indeed, my work in the last five years has been all about promoting the evolution of CSR from defensive, charitable and promotional modes to more strategic and transformative approaches – what I call CSR 2.0. Despite these efforts, and those of the ISO 26000 standard on social responsibility, it seems that if the label doesn't change, it is hard to change people's preconceptions and habits.

The second shift I have noticed is away from CSR and towards sustainability as a more holistic practice, as well as alternative conceptions such as Michael Porter and Mark Kramer's notion of creating shared value (CSV), or what myself and Chad Kymal are now calling creating integrated value (CIV). The change in language may seem like semantics, but it signals a change in thinking, which is important. In essence, the management of social, environmental and ethical issues is moving from the periphery (as a nice-to-have, optional extra) to the core of business (as a must-have, strategic imperative).

The third shift I am observing is that sustainable business is becoming less about compliance and risk management and more about breakthrough opportunities and innovation management. On the one hand, we see the rise of eco-innovation, being strongly promoted by the European Commission, OECD and UNEP, and on the other hand, the explosive growth of social entrepreneurship, with the catalytic support of institutions such as Ashoka, the Schwab Foundation and the Skoll Foundation. In effect, environmental and social challenges are being turned into market opportunities and we are looking not only to big corporates to bring solutions, but increasingly to creative, disruptive start-up ventures as well.

The combination of these three shifts convinced me to change the focus of the new World Guide, from corporate social responsibility to sustainable enterprise. Like *The World Guide to CSR*, this new edited collection brings together powerful summaries of the best academic research and practical cases on sustainable enterprise from countries around the world. However, unlike *The World Guide to CSR*, the emphasis is on sustainable business and social entrepreneurship, rather than traditional CSR and philanthropic approaches.

I define sustainable enterprise as any business, large or small, that integrates sustainability and responsibility, which includes value creation, good governance, societal contribution and ecological integrity, into its strategy, operations and products, in order to have a transformational, positive impact on the biggest social and environmental challenges we face.

The emphasis on sustainable enterprise, rather than corporate social responsibility, means that we are looking especially at innovative practices, including social enterprises, eco-entrepreneurs and companies that are introducing sustainable products and services into the market. We want to showcase companies and projects that are bringing disruptive solutions to our global challenges, rather than code-compliance or incremental change.

Sustainable enterprises are typically businesses that are practising five principles: creativity (innovation, entrepreneurship), scalability (designing solutions that can be applied to the mass market), responsiveness (using their business to directly tackle global social and environmental challenges), glocality (adopting global best practices, while maintaining local adaptation and sensitivity) and circularity (embracing zero-waste, closed-loop, cradle-to-cradle production).

Sustainable enterprise has also evolved from being a largely Western, developed-country phenomenon to being a diverse, "glocal" practice, with rapid take-up and many exciting innovations coming from developing countries and economies in transition. So I am especially pleased that we have 101 countries and eight regions profiled across the four volumes of *The World Guide to Sustainable Enterprise* – including 21 countries in Volume 2: Asia–Pacific.

My hope is that, in the coming five years, the sustainable enterprise movement will continue to spread around the world and to evolve into more transformative practices. We desperately need to reinvent capitalism to help smooth the transition to a low-carbon, more equitable and sustainable society. Sustainable enterprise can – indeed, must – be an integral part of this economic revolution. The alternative is a world in a state of perpetual crisis and collapse, where business is cast as the arch villain. Let us choose instead a more positive future – one that is safe, smart, sustainable, shared and satisfying – where business responsibility and innovation are a source of solutions and a beacon of light.

Wayne Visser
Cambridge, UK
December 2015

Part 1: Regional profiles

1

Central, East and South Asia

Aparna Mahajan
Director, Resource Mobilization and Partnerships, S M Sehgal Foundation, India

Regional context

Central Asia, comprising five independent republics, Kazakhstan, Kyrgyzstan, Uzbekistan, Turkmenistan and Tajikistan, is strategically positioned, acting as a bridge between Europe and Asia. About 90 million people, or 2% of Asia's total population, reside in Central Asia. Historically, Central Asia has been at the crossroads between different civilizations, largely because of the Silk Route which passed through this region, connecting Europe, West, South and East Asia. Central Asia is an extremely large region of varied geography, including high passes, mountains, deserts and grassy steppes. The majority of people earn a living by herding livestock, while economic centres are located in the major cities of the five countries. Central Asia has great potential to become an important trade corridor, particularly for small and medium enterprises.

About 38% of the population of Asia and 22% or over one-fifth of all the people in the world, live in East Asia. The region is one of the world's most populated places, ranking second in population only to South Asia. East Asia is home to some of the world's largest and most prosperous economies, such as China, Japan and the Democratic People's Republic of Korea. Rising exports have been a major source of domestic growth for most countries of the region. Although this region has witnessed remarkable growth in world trade and investment and is well positioned to become the largest regional market in the world, some economies such as Mongolia are still grappling with development challenges. East Asian countries are the principal beneficiaries of the massive increase in international private investment that is taking place.

South Asia, home to over one-fifth of the world's population, is the most populous and the most densely populated geographical region in the world. According to the UN's Multidimensional Poverty Index (MPI), just over a quarter of the world's MPI poor people live in Africa, while a half live in South Asia. According to the World Bank's ICP 2011 report, South Asia's share of the world's absolute poor was estimated at about 49% in 2005, but in 2011 it had declined to 29% due to record poverty declines in India.

India is by far the largest country in the subcontinent, covering around three-quarters of the land area and having largest population. It is also the world's largest democracy. According to the World Bank, 70% of the South Asian population and about 75% of South Asia's poor live in rural areas and most rely on agriculture for their livelihood. According to the Global Hunger Index, South Asia has one of the highest child malnutrition rates in the world.

Priority issues

Poverty, largely in rural areas in Asia, is a major issue, which is exacerbated by climate change. More than two-thirds of the world's poor people live in Asia, and nearly half of them are in South Asia. In some major countries, nearly 80% of poor people live in rural areas. While East Asia and South-East Asia have made impressive progress in reducing rural poverty over the past three decades, progress has been limited in South Asia. Poor rural households tend to have larger families, less education and higher levels of underemployment. They also lack basic amenities such as a safe water supply, sanitation and electricity and have limited access to credit, equipment and technology. Many poor rural households also suffer from landlessness or limited access to land.

In Central Asia, issues of rural poverty and food security are prominent and social and economic deprivation persists. For instance, high food and energy prices, combined with ineffective social protection systems and deteriorating Russian-era infrastructure, have left millions of households vulnerable to food insecurity and with limited access to reliable, affordable heating, electricity and basic services, particularly in the winter. These problems are exacerbated by the consequences of mismanagement of land and water resources and pollution, which have placed new strains on local economies, livelihood opportunities and ecosystems. The global economic and financial crisis, along with climate change and volatile food prices, have had serious impacts on economic development in many countries in the Central Asian region.

By contrast, the economies of East Asia make up one of the most successful regions of the world. A high level of structural differentiation, functional specialization, and autonomy of the economic system from government is a major contributor to industrial and commercial growth and prosperity. East Asia has been at the centre of what has been called an "economic miracle". In the last three decades, poverty in the region has been reduced by about two-thirds. Gross Domestic Product has been growing by 7–10% each year and Gross National Income by about 7% per year. Of the roughly US$170 billion in private capital flows to all developing countries last year, US$100 billion (nearly 60%) went to East Asia. Agricultural growth has contributed significantly to this economic upturn, especially in those countries where an egalitarian distribution of land took place, and where macroeconomic policies were stable and trade policies relatively open. China is an outstanding example of this trend.

According to a World Bank report in 2007, South Asia is the least integrated region in the world; trade between South Asian states is only 2% of the region's combined GDP, compared with 20% in East Asia. Sri Lanka has the highest GDP per capita in the region, while Afghanistan has the lowest. India is the largest economy in the region (US$1.97 trillion) and makes up almost 82% of the South Asian economy. Water scarcity remains one key environmental challenge, besides pollution and other issues of climate change for the South Asian countries.

Trends

In Central Asia, Kyrgyzstan is in a better situation to establish social enterprises in the country. Although not many NGOs are active, the country still has a more robust NGO sector than Kazakhstan or Tajikistan and NGOs play a significant role in the development process of the country. Social entrepreneurs in Kyrgyzstan and Tajikistan mainly focus on social and economic development of vulnerable groups. Their main activities are employment and capacity-building opportunities, arts, crafts and tourism initiatives, technical and financial support, and policy advocacy. Some explicitly promote active citizenship and civil society, including among youth. These social enterprise initiatives seek to improve the lives of target groups through empowerment and connection to markets and services. Target groups include people with disabilities, women, youth, refugees/migrants, and rural populations. Some key problems facing social enterprises in this region are lack of public awareness, an unfavourable legal environment, no sharing of best practices between social enterprises, lack of networking and communication between organizations and a lack of systemic and coherent government support/strategy.

There are varying levels of growth of sustainable and social enterprises in Eastern countries. Social enterprises are booming in Japan, where a survey by their Ministry of Economy, Trade, and Industry estimates that social business is a US$2.4 billion industry in Japan, which covers over 8,000 companies. Women's participation and leadership in social sectors is also being encouraged by the Japanese government. Social enterprises and civil society in Japan have flourished in the wake of natural disasters, and according to Nana Watanabe, founder of the Japanese arm of social entrepreneurship foundation Ashoka, it was the Great Hanshin (Kobe) earthquake in 1995 that first really mobilized civil society in Japan. Now there are many initiatives providing education for children and care for isolated elderly people in the disaster-stricken areas.

In China, on other hand, social enterprises are at a nascent stage (Zhao, 2012). Following the 2008 Sichuan earthquake and the expeditious response to the disaster by social entrepreneurs and non-profit organizations, social entrepreneurship increased in prominence. Since then, the sector and its advocates – incubators, impact investors, the media and academic researchers – have expanded across the country. Despite the various challenges social entrepreneurs face in China, an increasing number of social enterprises such as Shokay, Miaolosophy, Beijing LangLang Learning Potential Development Center and Canyou, are slowly emerging (BSR, 2012).

In South Korea, the Korea Social Enterprise Promotion Agency has been established to promote social enterprises. According to the Agency, a total of 850 social enterprises have obtained governmental authorization since the Social Enterprise Promotion Act was put into effect. Additionally,

2,000 new cooperatives were established in 2013. There has also been a growing number of intermediary organizations to help new social enterprises with mentoring, consulting and incubating services, such as the Social Enterprise Support Network, Seeds and the Korean Social Enterprise Promotion Agency.

In Mongolia, social enterprises are growing. Examples include: Nomsys, an internet providing company in the Gher districts of Ulaan Baatar; Righteous Living, a business that makes Ghers (traditional Mongolian houses) and that employs and assists Mongolians in need; Suu Milk, a dairy company that obtains milk from Mongolian nomadic herders; Mary & Martha Mongolia, a fair-trade company (certified by the World Fair Trade Organization) primarily focusing on hand crafted gifts made by Mongolian and Mongolian ethnic Kazakhs; Gateway Development, manufacturer of insulated building material in Mongolia, which can significantly reduce the cost of heating in Mongolia (with over seven months of severe winter where the temperature can drop below –50°C, Mongolia lacks innovative ways to reduce energy usage during winter); and Nemer International LLC, a water resources management company that works to advocate responsible water usage in Mongolia.

In South Asia, sustainable and social enterprises have been on the rise with social enterprises having grown spectacularly in India. The country has been referred to as "a social enterprise superpower" by Think, a social action think-tank and action hub, as well as "a hotbed for social enterprise" by *Beyond Profit* magazine (Poon, 2011). Over the last decade, the scope of social enterprises and impact investors in India has expanded and key sectors include agriculture, education, energy, financial services, healthcare, housing, sanitation, and water. According to the *Beyond Profit* 2010 survey, about 68% of social enterprises in India have been in existence for five years or less (Asian Development Bank, 2012). A growing trend is the transformation of many not-for-profit models into for-profit models. Examples include: Pipal Tree Ventures Private Limited, which trains rural youth in various construction and infrastructure-related skills and has found a way for rural youth to get out of poverty; and International Development Enterprises, which has helped pull millions of small farmers out of poverty in India.

In Pakistan, the social enterprise landscape is nascent but fast-growing. In a 2013 report called "Enterprising Pakistan" by the British Council in collaboration with the YES Network Pakistan, social entrepreneurship in the areas of health, environment and skills is highlighted. The Economic Policy

Group report entitled "Social Entrepreneurship in Pakistan: Unlocking Innovation Through Enterprise Incubation" explains how incubator hubs can unlock the innovation potential of Pakistan's social entrepreneurs, highlighting successful incubator models already in existence at some of Pakistan's premier business schools (Shah and Shubhisham, 2013).

Government policies

In Central Asia, the Association of Social Entrepreneurs (ASE) was registered as a legal entity in April 2012 in Kyrgyzstan and represents the first attempt to associate a network of organizations. While there is legislation in Kyrgyzstan that provides tax incentives for charitable organizations, there are significant barriers to entry that have negated the impact of the legislation. The Philanthropy law (1999) states that any NGO can re-register as a charitable organization if they spend 98% of their income on charity (meaning only 2% can be spent on all operational costs including rent and salaries). Under such strict conditions, not a single organization has registered as a charitable organization since the law was passed.

Another law relates to Not-for-Profit Agencies (1999), which governs the registration and operations of all NGOs in Kyrgyzstan. However, the National Tax Code administers economic activity of NGOs separately. There is a draft law on Charitable Organizations and Charitable Activity which aims to increase the role of charitable organizations in social life, to stimulate and enhance efficiency of their public benefit activity, and to set high standards of management, transparency and accountability to society. There is another law on Social Order (2008), which aims to improve the efficiency of state funds allocated to socioeconomic needs and to improve the quality of the country's social services. Under this law, the Ministry of Labour and Social Protection allocates funds to NGOs (via a tender process) for improving the social environment and for solving social issues in the communities (USAID and Synergos, 2013).

In Tajikistan, there is a National Tax Code, which regulates the taxation system for all legal entities, including the economic activities of NGOs. There is a law on Charitable Activity (2003), which provides a detailed explanation about what types of organization, activity and programme should be considered as charitable. This law also describes the nature of

Charitable Foundations that provide needed support to the marginalized people of the country.

In East Asia, among the major policy choices commonly adopted are openness to foreign trade, significant levels of government savings and an emphasis on education. Government intervention has played an important role in East Asian economies. To varying degrees, East Asian economies maintained significant tariff and non-tariff barriers through much of their initial rapid growth periods and also adopted industrial policies, in varying degrees, to support selected industries.

In South Korea, the Social Enterprise Promotion Act was approved in December 2006 and was put into effect in July 2007. The Ministry of Labour is obliged to "establish the Basic Plan for Social Enterprises Support" every five years (Article 5). In terms of this law, not only companies but also cooperatives and non-profit organizations can be recognized as social enterprises, which are eligible for tax relief and/or financial support from the Korean national or provincial governments or city councils. 680 entities have been recognized as social enterprises as of October 2012. The majority of Korean social enterprises are primarily concerned with job creation.

South Asia is influenced by a major policy convergence. The policies of India and the nearby countries of ASEAN, are all pro-economic growth, pro-international trade, and generally against tensions and conflicts that may inhibit trade and growth. These policies are backed by commitments by governments to economic liberalization at home, and to achieving high economic growth through market-oriented methods. Social enterprises aim to provide high-quality yet affordable goods and services such as healthcare, education, and financial services to the poor, thus creating social benefits while making a profit.

As a clear validation of the power of social innovation, the Government of India announced an Rs.1,000 crore National Innovation Fund to support ideas to address developmental needs in education, health, infrastructure and sanitation. One of the recent landmark laws in India is Section 135 of the new Companies Act 2013, which states that with effect from 1 April 2014, every company, private limited or public limited, which either has a net worth of Rs.500 crore or a turnover of Rs.1,000 crore or net profit of Rs.5 crore, needs to spend at least 2% of its average net profit for the immediately preceding three financial years on corporate social responsibility activities.

Case studies

Golden Sun (China)

Golden Sun offers a range of support services and emergency assistance to a network of over 30,000 elderly residents of Fuzhou. Launched in 2007, it describes its mission as a "Nursing Home Without Walls" and seeks to provide high-quality care for the elderly at low cost. Each member of its network is provided with a mobile phone and can call Golden Sun's 24-hour hotline to access a range of services. These include assistance with shopping and food delivery, home cleaning services, companionship and medical consultations, as well as emergency assistance if members are ill, in danger or lost. The call centre receives 5,000 calls per month. The phones are connected to a satellite positioning system so that if a member calls in distress, staff at Golden Sun can contact the emergency services and direct them to the right place.

In addition to its call centre, Golden Sun operates 89 community centres in Fuzhou. Its staff included retired care professionals, doctors, nurses, housekeepers and volunteers. At present, Golden Sun serves around 30% of all pensioners in Fuzhou and all residents over 85. Most receive membership as part of their retirement package and for those who pay, the fees are means-tested so even those on low incomes can join. Golden Sun has enjoyed rapid growth and formed partnerships with China Telecom, Ping An Insurance and Xiamen Bank and secured angel investment (typically the earliest equity investments made in startup companies by wealthy individuals) as well as local government support.

Hanbit Art Company (South Korea)

This art company develops performance art among the handicapped by discovering and fostering their talents. For example, through the performances of the blind concert orchestra, the art company improves the recognition of the handicapped, while providing vulnerable social groups with jobs and social services. By working with local residents, it aims to promote economic stability and self-reliance, while adding to their quality of life by providing cultural activities.

Hathay Bunano Proshikhan Samity (HBPS) (Bangladesh)

This social enterprise employs female Bangladeshi artisans to produce children's toys and clothes that are sold in Australia, the USA, the UK and other European nations. Through this organization, which was launched in 2005, women are able to obtain economic freedom and rural employment opportunities without any debt. While many NGOs in Bangladesh try to generate employment for the poor through microcredit, HBPS chose to provide direct employment opportunities for poor women in rural areas, with special preference given to disadvantaged groups. Since 2005, the company has been producing hand-crocheted and hand-knitted children's toys and clothes. The working model of HBPS is based on a low-cost, labour intensive, electricity-saving, low technology production process and leverages the women's capabilities.

HBPS benefits from the leadership of its founders, a British-Bangladeshi couple, and the financial support of multinational corporations, international development agencies and local NGOs. It relies on local leaders to obtain information about the local workforce and infrastructure, and to raise awareness. The growth of HBPS has been quite phenomenal, with employment and revenue almost doubling every year. In 2009, HBPS had 54 centres and 3,500 employees. Beginning with an initial investment of US$500, it is now generating a sales volume of about 120,000 pieces per year, and a profit margin of 42%, which is reinvested into the business for training, marketing, research, and other development purposes.

Social Enterprise English Language School (SEELS) (Japan)

SEELS is a social enterprise that provides innovative and compelling English-language teaching services operated by under-served Filipino migrants as certified teachers. It targets residential areas with middle- and low-income brackets and plans to scale up and replicate its micro-franchising model to untapped residential areas where under-supported families reside. Akira Foundation Japan works collaboratively with SEELS to foster an inclusive community-based culture for both Filipino migrants and lower-income families in Japan. SEELS offers its services at very low cost, compared with existing traditional English schools common near train stations or around major cities. Most of its teachers have been under-served Filipino migrants living in Japan and will be certified through a high-quality teaching-learning method, dubbed the Community and Home Based English Teachers (CHOBET) training programme, in collaboration with the national network of Filipino English Teacher in Japan (FETJ).

Akira Foundation provided Mr Cesar Santoyo, Executive Director of the Center for Japanese-Filipino Families (CJFF) and President of SEELS, with a start-up grant for registration fees and "patient loans" for seed capital. Akira Foundation has been progressively supporting SEELS in terms of operational and strategic management so that it would evolve into a successful and sustainable social enterprise, while addressing dual social and economic issues between the Philippines and Japan at a new level of collaborative and humanitarian approaches.

"This partnership is a key to Akira Foundation's effort to raise awareness of insidious social issues in Japan and realize one of the two pillars in our mission statement: to promote social entrepreneurship as a bridge between Japan and the Global Village," said Hirofumi Yokoi. "We will invest the necessary resources to make SEELS grow and sustain, while supporting it to create significant opportunities for Filipino migrants and lower-income families in Japan to gain more confidence and independence, both financially and socially."

Waterlife (India)

Groundwater quality is poor in India; around 85% of rural households do not have access to safe quality water for consumption. Major contaminants include microbacteria, fluoride, arsenic, iron, salt and nitrate. $1.5 billion is spent annually on rural medical expenses, of which $600 million is due to water-borne diseases. Waterlife addresses this gap by installing and maintaining water purification plants that purify water from various sources such as surface water (lakes and ponds), groundwater and pressurized flows (municipal supplies) in each village.

Waterlife minimizes business risk by having multiple revenue streams including sales of equipment, water and maintenance contracts. Waterlife also has two types of purification plant: community water systems (high-capacity units for dense villages) and customized contaminants removal units (lower-capacity units to tackle specific impurities). Additionally, Waterlife works on establishing infrastructure for water distribution in villages. Their major revenue streams are equipment sales to the government and water sales to consumers.

Waterlife had a successful start which can be attributed to the experience of the management team in both multinational organizations and start-ups in the water market. Within two years of inception, it has achieved financial and operational break-even while also attracting investment from Aavishkaar, the micro-venture fund. Waterlife plans to reach ten states in the next year alone, and focus on government projects in the next few years. Already it has provided safe water to 1.1 million people through 1,300 installations in four states and saved over 50,000 people in more than 250 villages of West Bengal last year from falling prey to arsenicosis, a contaminated water-borne disease that may cause skin cancer.

Further resources

Alliance for Social Entrepreneurship – A three-year collaborative programme aimed at creating and supporting a robust social entrepreneurship movement in selected developing countries, including Kyrgyzstan and Tajikistan. Formed by the US Agency for International Development (USAID) and the Synergos Institute in collaboration with Ashoka and the Schwab Foundation for Social Entrepreneurship, the Alliance will work with leading organizations active in social entrepreneurship globally and in select countries.

Asia–Pacific Centre for Sustainable Enterprise – Established at Griffiths University to inform and assist the development of sustainable enterprise through innovative research, teaching and engagement activities.

Association of Social Entrepreneurs of Kyrgyzstan – A public organization that unites successful social entrepreneurs to unify their voices and efforts towards social wellbeing through the development of social entrepreneurship and public–private partnerships.

Sankalp Forum – A global platform for social enterprises, with a mission to create an enabling platform that supports socially relevant small and medium-sized enterprises. The Forum provides year-round access to investment opportunities, capacity building, knowledge and crucial networks. It connects over 400 social enterprises, over 400 investors and funders, and 10,000 other stakeholders from across the world. Sankalp Forum in an initiative by Intellecap, a social advisory firm that works in under-served markets. The Sankalp Awards attract applications from the most innovative, scalable and sustainable enterprises across India.

Social Enterprise Network Asia – Aims to promote the sustainable growth of the social enterprise sector in Asia, especially by providing innovative and scalable solutions to the increasingly complex challenges in this region. The Network offers a social enterprise platform, generating know-how, building capacity, improving access to the market and mobilizing social finance. Members are from Indonesia, Japan, Malaysia, Philippines, Singapore, Thailand and Vietnam.

References

Asian Development Bank (2012). *India social enterprise landscape report*. Manilla: ADB.
BSR (2012). *China social enterprise report 2012*. San Francisco: Business for Social Responsibility.
Poon, D. (2011). The emergence and development of social enterprise sectors. *Social Impact Research Experience Journal* (SIRE), Working paper, Wharton School.
Shah, P. & Shubhisham, S. (2013). *Social enterprise in Pakistan: unlocking innovation through enterprise incubation*. London: EPG.
USAID & Synergos (2013). Mapping social entrepreneurship in Kyrgyzstan and Tajikistan. A Report to the Alliance for Social Entrepreneurship under project Strengthening Social Entrepreneurship and Civil Society in Central Asia, September.
Zhao, M. (2012). The social enterprise emerges in China. *Stanford Social Innovation Review*, Spring.

II
South-East Asia and Oceania

Jeremy B. Williams
Director, Asia Pacific Centre for Sustainable Enterprise, Griffith University, Australia

Regional context

According to the Human Development Index (HDI) (UNDP, 2013), the majority of states in the South-East Asia and Oceania regions are classified as "medium" in terms of the level of their development. Among the outliers are Australia, New Zealand, and Singapore with "very high" human development, and Myanmar (Burma), Papua New Guinea and the Solomon Islands with "low" human development. The broad similarity in the level of development aside, there is considerable diversity within this grouping on a number of dimensions. For example, there is a rich country with an island continent all to itself, together with quite a large number of Small Island Developing States (SIDS). There are countries with large populations and some with small. There are some nations that are resource-rich and some that are resource-poor. There are some established liberal democracies and other countries that are emerging from periods under military dictatorships or state socialism. All of these varying influences can have a bearing on one's perspective and commitment to sustainable enterprise.

In terms of the geopolitics of the region, Australia holds considerable sway. There has been a long-standing free trade agreement with New Zealand in the form of Closer Economic Relations (CER), and both countries have historical ties with Pacific island nations through the Pacific

Islands Forum. Australia's population is around twice that of the other 15 members combined and its economy is more than five times larger. Both Australia and New Zealand have been significant aid donors in the past, and they provide key export markets for the other Pacific countries. Meanwhile, economic integration with the countries comprising the Association of South-East Asian Nations (ASEAN) has also been facilitated with the establishment of the ASEAN–Australia–New Zealand Free Trade Area (AANZFTA). The Agreement came into effect in 2010 for eight of its signatories: Australia, Brunei, Malaysia, Myanmar, New Zealand, Singapore, the Philippines and Vietnam. Thailand followed in 2010, Laos and Cambodia in 2011, and Indonesia in 2012.

Greater economic integration invariably leads to greater political cooperation, and this has led to greater diplomatic efforts in recent years on the part of governments throughout the region. Australia, in particular, has been keen to engage with countries in the Asia–Pacific region on the basis of partnership and mutual respect, rather than in the guise of regional hegemon. The publication of the *Australia in the Asian Century* White Paper (Commonwealth of Australia, 2012) provided, perhaps, the most clearly articulated vision by an Australian government in this regard when it was released in October 2012, with 25 national objectives to be achieved by 2015.

Interestingly, "National Objective 7" focuses on how natural capital (environmental assets) will need to be managed sustainably to ensure the well-being of future generations. There is also reference (section 5.8: "Charting a sustainable course") to the growing demand for non-renewable resources in the region and how this must not come at the expense of ecological sustainability. This would likely have resonated with many other countries within the grouping, particularly those most vulnerable to the effects of climate change (Intergovernmental Panel on Climate Change (IPCC), 2014). Tuvalu, for example, could be one of the first to request that Australia welcome part of its population on a permanent basis when they become "displaced persons" due to rising sea levels (Farbotko and Lazrus, 2012). It is worth noting that semantics are important here. The Tuvalese and others in SIDS shy away from being described as potential "climate refugees"; a reflection, perhaps, of the controversy surrounding refugee status in Australia under the government led by Tony Abbott.

Priority issues

As far as priority issues in the region are concerned it is very difficult to look beyond the impact of climate change. The Intergovernmental Panel on Climate Change (IPCC) (2014) in its Fifth Assessment Report (AR5) states, quite unequivocally, that left unchecked climate change could spiral out of control leading to dire consequences for all living things on the planet. Not surprisingly, the IPCC implores world leaders to sign a new climate agreement at the Paris meeting of the United Nations Framework Convention on Climate Change (UNFCCC) Conference of the Parties (COP21) in December 2015.

The increasing frequency of extreme weather events such as cyclones in the Philippines, bush-fires in Australia and floods in Thailand, has led to an increased focus on climate adaptation and building resilience. This is a major challenge for all countries in the region, but nowhere more than in the Pacific, where some low-lying islands are already facing major problems as a result of rising sea levels.

The vulnerability of SIDS to sea-level rise is amplified on account of their relatively small landmasses, population concentrations, and high dependence on coastal ecosystems for their livelihoods. Sea-level rises will vary widely by region, in accordance with prevailing winds, ocean currents, and the gravitational pull of the polar ice sheets. As a result, some coastal areas will be inundated while others could remain dry. In the Oceania region the outlook is not good. While the global average sea-level rise is 3.2 mm per year, the island of Kosrae, in the Federated States of Micronesia, is experiencing sea-level rise at a rate of 10 mm per year. Meanwhile, in the western Pacific, where a large number of small islands are located, recorded sea-level rises between 1993 and 2009 were around four times the global average at a rate of 12 mm per year (UNEP, 2014).

South-East Asia's exposure to climate change risk may not be as acutely existential as low-lying islands in the Pacific, but as the 2015 Climate Change and Environmental Risk Atlas (CCERA) published by global risk analytics company Maplecroft documents, there are countries in this region that are identified as facing "extreme risk" in the Climate Change Vulnerability Index (CCVI), including the Philippines (ranked the eighth highest risk globally), Cambodia (12th) and Myanmar (19th) (Maplecroft, 2014).

Climate adaptation on the part of proactive organizations is a key to mitigating risk. Certainly, the improved understanding of the science and projected consequences of climate change – as highlighted by the IPCC AR5 – offers hope that adaptation strategies can be developed to avoid the worst impacts (Intergovernmental Panel on Climate Change (IPCC), 2014). Investment in sustainable enterprise can be a key driver in this regard, through the development of more resilient infrastructure, economic activities that restore natural capital, and initiatives that serve to reduce poverty.

Trends

It has become increasingly apparent that to live and work in a sustainable society we need sustainable enterprise to create economic, ecological and social value. Indeed, given that a number of the planetary boundaries that define a safe operating space for humankind have already been transgressed (Rockström *et al.*, 2009), we need these organizations to do more than just do no harm to ecosystems and society, we need them to behave in a way that restores and protects natural and social capital.

Sustainable enterprise is essentially an outgrowth of corporate social responsibility (CSR) – and what started out as an "add-on" is now becoming an integral part of organizational strategy; at least for forward-looking organizations. For these companies, it is a necessary transition as – confronted with increasing risk because of climate change – their continued operation depends on it. This outlook is rapidly becoming the mainstream view as investors and other stakeholders see obvious value creation and cost reduction opportunities in the strategic use of sustainability concepts and practices.

In the South-East Asia and Oceania regions, there is growing awareness that sustainability is a critical component of the larger socio-ecological system and is therefore something to be encouraged. In this regard, there is active interventionism on the part of the state in some instances, and in others it is largely driven by private enterprise or non-governmental organizations (NGOs). In terms of good practice for others to emulate, it is still very early days. To begin with, the concept of sustainability itself is subject to multiple interpretations, some of which might have little to do with the socio-ecological system. Second, even when organizations do have a clear understanding of their role in the creation of economic, environmental and social value, the focus tends to be on becoming less unsustainable, rather than on a future state of complete sustainability.

This might appear a trivial distinction to make, but it is indicative of the fact that the vast majority of organizations are just setting out on their sustainability journey. Those leading the charge – or grabbing the limelight at least – are the larger corporates operating in Australia and Singapore. According to the *2014 Global 100*, an index of the most sustainable companies in the world maintained by Corporate Knights (2014), the Australian banking corporation WestPac is the most sustainable corporation in the world. Other notable entries include ANZ (19th), and the Commonwealth Bank of Australia (25th), all of whom are not beyond criticism given that their lending practices sanction loans to highly unsustainable enterprises, including clients within the fossil fuel industry.

Unilever, meanwhile, ranked a lowly 93rd in this index and the likes of Puma and Patagonia did not rank at all, when all three companies are consistently regarded as being among the trailblazers in the corporate sustainability arena. Unilever Asia, for example, was recognized as the most sustainable business operating in Singapore at the 2014 Sustainable Business Awards. Known for its "Sustainable Living Plan" initiative, Unilever has a blueprint for sustainability based on three main goals: improving health and wealth being, reducing environmental impact and enhancing livelihoods, including a commitment to end deforestation in its supply chain. The company is highly regarded for its community engagement and commitment to sustainable agriculture by sourcing raw materials from certified sources, particularly for its tea and ice cream brands. It was chosen as the overall winner for its robust management system in tracking the progress of its sustainability goals, which are embedded within its business strategy.

The central point here is that sustainability rankings sometimes cannot be taken at face value. Evaluation criteria can vary quite dramatically to the point where it is quite possible for an oil company to rank highly. A truly sustainable enterprise will be driven by a compelling sustainability vision accompanied by the monitoring of performance relative to that vision. It is difficult, therefore, for a company engaged in or closely associated with fossil fuel production to meaningfully talk about their sustainability vision unless they have a plan to transition out of fossil fuels to renewable energy production. In short, business as usual with some CSR tacked on the end is no longer an option because this is not compatible with sustainable development.

Much of the literature on sustainable business practices in South-East Asia and Oceania has naturally concentrated on the large, multinational companies (MNCs), whose impacts are significant, even if the focus tends to be on how much less unsustainable they are, rather than how much closer they are to becoming truly sustainable. The really exciting trend – yet to be documented in any meaningful way – is the emergence of sustainability entrepreneurs who are identifying social-ecological problems as opportunities for establishing sustainable enterprise. These start-ups are more easily established in the developing countries of South-East Asia and the Pacific than in Australia or New Zealand where the service economies are more reliant on fossil fuels and material consumption. Some countries in the region, such as Cambodia, Indonesia and Vietnam, for example, are actively encouraging the development of "green economies" that encourage local businesses and companies to develop sustainable practices at the outset.

Government policies

In stark contrast to the public policy settings in Australia, where the government is actively winding back initiatives that encourage sustainable enterprise, other countries in the South-East Asia and Oceania regions are doing a lot to incentivize the emergence of a new, green economy.

In South-East Asia in particular, "green growth" has become a central theme for a number of the emerging countries in the region. It is seen as an alternative pathway to development that avoids environmental degradation, loss of biodiversity, and unsustainable use of natural resources. The United Nations Economic and Social Commission for Asia and the Pacific (ESCAP) has been a leading advocate of the green growth concept with the policy focus being environmentally sustainable economic progress that fosters low-carbon, socially inclusive development. The Organisation for Economic Co-operation and Development (OECD) has also been a key protagonist. In a recent report, *Towards Green Growth in Southeast Asia*, it highlighted that South-East Asia has a golden opportunity to leapfrog the low-performing, polluting, and resource-inefficient technologies of more developed economies, forgoing the "grow-now-and-clean-up-later" model that has proven so disastrous (OECD, 2014, p. 3). Instead, there is an opportunity to pursue a far-sighted, green growth strategy that will safeguard the wellbeing of future generations.

The Cambodian government, for example, has embraced the idea of green growth with great alacrity. In March 2013, it launched the national policy and strategic plan for green growth, 2013–30. The plan incorporates inclusive and sustainable policies that aim to strengthen and expand local democracy and promote local development, focusing on four areas including agricultural development, infrastructure, private-sector engagement and human capital development. The approach is "people-centred" and not solely focused on growth in GDP or income (Mohammed *et al.*, 2013, pp. 13-14).

The development of sustainable enterprise in Cambodia is thus a very top-down affair. The Government creates the conditions and framework to stimulate a green economy and does not leave much to self-regulation in what is essentially an under-developed private business sector. It pushes the adoption of sustainable enterprise practices through a mix of taxation measures, legislation and direct investment. An example is direct incentives to protect ecosystem services (Mohammed *et al.*, 2013, p. 22).

In October 2013, the Indonesian government – supported by the Global Green Growth Institute (GGGI) – released their first joint report entitled "Prioritizing Investments: Delivering Green Growth" (GoI-GGGI, 2013). The report highlights that, among other things, renewable energy is a major element in the development of a green economy. Government policies aim to decrease greenhouse gas emissions by reducing dependence on fossil fuels, and cutting the associated fuel subsidies. The aim is to change its energy mix and, by 2025, have at least 15% of the country's energy generated from renewable sources. The government is seeking to meet this aim through direct investment in clean energy sources, and also through payment for ecosystems services via the UN REDD+ programme (Reducing Emissions from Deforestation and forest Degradation).

More recently, the Vietnamese Ministry of Planning and Investment announced a National Action Plan on Green Growth. The aim of this plan, launched in April 2014, is to accelerate the process of economic restructuring towards the efficient use of natural resources, the reduction of greenhouse gas emissions through research and application of modern technologies, and the development of infrastructure to improve the economy and reduce poverty. Once again, this is a top-down approach but not uncharacteristic of what has historically been a command economy. The role of business and industry in changing economic and production practices has been recognized, however, with the Vietnamese government expressing its desire to encourage foreign investment in the development of a green and sustainable economy. The Vietnam Business Council for Sustainable Development (VBCSD) – official global network partner of the World Business Council for Sustainable Development – is a lead agency in implementing the National Action Plan and includes among its membership companies such as Unilever that can share experiences with smaller Vietnamese businesses.

Case studies

Bankmecu (Australia)

Bankmecu is the first bank in Australia to take a responsible approach to banking with the aim of meeting the economic, social and environmental performance expectations of its customers. It operates under the same set of prudential standards that apply to all other Australian banks, but is based on a cooperative business model in which each customer is a shareholder of the bank. With this single share, every customer has an equal opportunity to say how the bank should be run.

Profits are reinvested back into the bank to provide customers with lower fees, better interest rates and the quality of service they expect. In addition, up to 4% of the Bank's after tax profit is allocated to a range of community and environmental projects that customers indicate are important to them such as social housing, investment in community resilience, environmental sustainability, and the financial and governance capabilities of not-for-profit organizations. This initiative is a direct response to the desire for a broader measure of "progress" in the community other than economic growth alone.

In summary, besides ensuring its business operations are sustainable, Bankmecu believes it also has a responsibility to support its customers in their efforts to live more sustainably.

Biomax (Singapore)

Biomax Technologies converts organic waste into 100% pure certified organic fertilizer within 24 hours. The technology, called the Rapid Thermophilic Digestion System, offers a simple solution for businesses looking to dispose of organic wastes. The company has developed specially formulated enzymes containing a variety of naturally occurring microorganisms that operate under thermophilic conditions in a specially designed digester to break down complex organic compounds into simpler organic matter at an unprecedented speed.

The Biomax digester can operate on various energy sources with high durability, efficiencies and minimal maintenance. It is an enclosed system and the organic wastes are treated in a way that produces a very consistent output that is odourless and pathogen free, with no harmful by-products. The system can accommodate agricultural wastes such as sugarcane, palm oil and grain husks; livestock wastes including animal manure, egg processing and slaughtering; and municipal wastes from food, horticulture and waste-water sludge.

As a sustainable enterprise, Biomax is a prime example of industrial ecology in practice. It eliminates organic waste without harming the environment, reduces landfill, and produces a high-quality organic fertilizer as a substitute for chemically based fertilizers, for which there is a growing market given growing concerns about bio-security.

G-Energy Solutions (Papua New Guinea)

Commencing operations in 2013, the core business of G-Energy Solutions is as a service provider to assist clients in Papua New Guinea and the Solomon Islands to monitor and control their energy usage. The key technology is called Eniscope, a British product that combines advanced smart metering and real-time energy displays to show exactly how much energy is being used and what is using it.

Prospective customers can take advantage of a free energy survey, and then G-Energy Solutions makes recommendations on the best course of action comprising customized training programmes to raise awareness and motivation to reduce energy costs. They also offer a comprehensive energy audit aimed at identifying all opportunities for low-cost or zero-cost energy solutions, and information on the investments that would need to be made and their corresponding payback periods.

Businesses such as G-Energy Solutions are quite rare in this part of the world, even when the scope for savings from energy efficiency measures are large, because discretionary investment expenditure levels tend to be more constrained than in developed countries. However, with government funding assistance and innovative pay-as-you-save type financing programmes, the opportunities for this type of sustainable enterprise are considerable.

Green School Bali (Indonesia)

Founded in 2008, Green School is probably the best example in the world of a school as a sustainable enterprise. Set on 20 acres, the school's buildings are constructed entirely from bamboo, lalang-alang grass (a local grass), and mud bricks employing a sophisticated architectural design. The campus is powered through renewable energy sources such as solar power, biogas and micro-hydropower from the river. The ecological footprint of the school is close to zero as it functions in perfect harmony with its environs, and uses an organic permaculture system – cultivated and managed by the students – to provide a source of food and a sink for recycling waste.

Green School seeks to educate young leaders in global citizenship, championing a new model of learning with an intimate connection to nature. It is preparing students to be critical and creative thinkers, equipping them with the knowledge and the confidence to make a real difference in the way we manage the planet. Being at one with nature – in classrooms without walls – has had a hugely positive impact on student learning. There are plenty of distractions at Green School but they are natural distractions that are compatible and not in conflict with the learning process.

Sailing for Sustainability (Fiji)

Sailing for Sustainability is an action research project that arose out of rising fuel costs that were crippling the economy of Fiji – a nation of 300 islands – as ferry services and interisland trade became uneconomic. With some prompting from Sailing for Sustainability and the Fijian Island Voyaging Society (FIVS), it was decided that the best option might be to delve back into the past and draw on the traditional maritime prowess of Pacific nations. Known and respected as skilled ocean voyagers, the knowledge built up over generations has been almost forgotten in the recent years.

Ironically, the performance of Fijian ocean craft known as "Drua" or "Vaqa" was considered by Captain Cook to be far superior to any other sailing boat in existence. They could carry more people and freight than any European vessel and were three times faster. Now it is believed that these ancient technologies could be adapted for Fiji and other Pacific island nations to develop the first alternative shipping network in the world.

In the first instance, however, the vision is to connect all Pacific islands in a sustainable, carbon-neutral way that would deliver energy independence, better infrastructure and more economic opportunities for remote island communities.

Further resources

Green Cross Australia – Through its business and research partnerships Green Cross Australia draws together like-minded leaders and their companies and research institutions towards a vision of a more resilient Australia. Its Business Adaptation Network, for example, provides an industry forum to support learning, build capacity, and promote and recognize best practice in climate change adaptation.

Impact Investment Exchange Asia (IIX) – Operates the Impact Incubator and Impact Partners platforms to help social enterprises access impact investment capital in private transactions. IIX also launched Impact Exchange, the world's first social stock exchange.

SharingValueAsia – A platform based in Thailand to develop and showcase partnership and corporate-led solutions forged between business leaders, policy-makers, NGOs and civil society. The initiative is supported by a number of corporations including HP, KKR, FleishmanHillard and Food Industry Asia, and NGOs including CARE, World Vision and Action Aid. SharingValueAsia is developing a fully indexed library of over 200 case studies from across the Asia–Pacific.

Sustainable Business Australia (SBA) – A not-for-profit membership-based organization that includes banking and finance, technology and infrastructure developers, consultancy and engineering companies. In 2014 it was appointed as the Australian Global Network partner for the World Business Council for Sustainable Development (WBCSD).

Sustainable Business Network (SBN) – A membership-based enterprise, made up of businesses, governmental agencies and organizations located across New Zealand. The SBN vision is to make New Zealand a model sustainable nation, focusing on four critical areas: enabling the use of renewable energy, building resilient communities, mega efficiency by maximizing the use of all resources, and through restoration of New Zealand's natural capital.

References

Commonwealth of Australia (2012). *Australia in the Asian Century*, White Paper, October. Canberra: Commonwealth of Australia.

Corporate Knights (2014). 2014 Global 100: An index of the Global 100 most sustainable corporations in the world. Toronto.

Farbotko, C., & Lazrus, H. (2012). The first climate refugees? Contesting global narratives of climate change in Tuvalu. *Global Environmental Change*, 22(2), 382-390.

GOI (Government of Indonesia) & GGGI (Global Green Growth Institute) (2013). *Prioritizing investment: delivering green growth*. Green Growth Program. Jakarta: Joint Secretariat GoI-GGGI Green Growth Program.

Intergovernmental Panel on Climate Change (IPCC) (2014). *Climate change 2014: synthesis report*. Geneva: IPCC.

Maplecroft (2014). Climate change and environmental risk atlas (CCERA). Bath: Maplecroft.

Mohammed, E.Y., Wang, S. & Kawaguchi, G. (2013). *Making growth green and inclusive: The case of Cambodia*, OECD Green Growth Papers. Paris: OECD.

OECD (Organisation for Economic Co-operation and Development) (2014). *Towards green growth in Southeast Asia*, OECD Green Growth Studies. Paris: OECD Publishing.

Rockström, J., Steffen, W., Noone, K., Persson, A., Chapin, F.S., Lambin, E.F., ... Foley, J.A. (2009). A safe operating space for humanity. *Nature*, 461, 472-475, 24 September, doi: 10.1038.461472a.

UNDP (United Nations Development Programme) (2013). *Human development report 2013: the rise of the south: human progress in a diverse world*. New York: UNDP.

UNEP (United Nations Environment Programme) (2014). *Emerging issues for small island developing states*. Results of the UNEP foresight process. Nairobi: UNEP.

Part 2: Country profiles

1
Australia

Colin Higgins
Senior Lecturer, Deakin Business School, Deakin University, Australia

Lauren James
Commercialisation and Vendor Assurance Manager, Fonterra Brands, Australia

National context

While corporate Australia has made a credible commitment to sustainability and corporate social responsibility, its transition towards sustainable enterprise is less encouraging. Australian business is predominantly focused on strategic CSR – where social and environmental issues are mitigated through risk management. Where sustainable enterprise is apparent, it is mostly among those seeking competitive differentiation through sustainability, or among social enterprises. On the whole, sustainable enterprise lacks integration within the business community and responsiveness, creativity and circularity (closed-loop/cradle-to-cradle) strategies are rare.

Despite facing some of the most extreme weather in the world, bearing the brunt of devastating natural disasters (such as floods and bush-fires), and an economy dependent on natural resources, business and government thinking about sustainability – and the transformations required – are immature. Government policy, based around commitments made following the Rio+20 summit in 2012, is largely about funding targeted initiatives in priority areas. These include sustainable management of oceans, poverty reduction among indigenous peoples, gender equality, food security, spreading the benefits of mining, and disaster risk reduction. Overlooked is any role for business. Business is expected to deliver economic sustainability, and is assumed to invest in cleaner technologies and undertake research and development into new products and services. Coordination of action that provides impetus to the necessary changes is sparse.

A vacuum in practitioner guidance and tools also hampers the development of sustainable enterprise. The Business Council of Australia and the Australian Industry Group are conservative in their views, while others struggle to attain a critical mass. The political climate hasn't helped. The 2007–13 Labour Government's climate policy was poorly implemented and became hostage to a weary electorate. The current Conservative Government (2013 onward) has laid out its priorities as fiscal responsibility, limited Government, and "affordable" environmental policy, commencing with the axing of the Climate Coalition. This was later resurrected through crowdfunding, proving a significant independent public support for this agenda.

Encouragingly for the integration and mainstreaming of sustainability was the acquisition of dominant international consultancy Ernst & Young and Net Balance in September 2014. Now cornering the sustainability market in Australia, this sparks a promising move for the advancement of sustainability in mainstream business.

While frameworks for action in Australia continue to hinge on "social licence to operate", all may not be lost in terms of grass-roots social entrepreneurship and innovation among some large companies. These remain exceptions rather than the norm.

Priority issues

Australia emerged from the global financial crisis relatively unscathed, but recent trends have delivered some economic uncertainty. Over dependence on commodities and resources and a semi-dependence on Asia will cause pain as China and India slow. A high Australian dollar has reduced competitiveness in manufacturing, retail and tourism sectors and a high comparative cost structure is leading to offshoring of some manufacturing and services.

Declining public finances and budget deficits are becoming important economic (and political) problems, as a strong commodity sector no
longer provides a cushion for the domestic economy. Addressing inequality
through indigenous economic development focusing on financial security,
entrepreneurship, education, and mining companies is also vulnerable to
economic rumbles (Australian Government, 2011).

Australia's society is rapidly ageing and digitizing. Australia cannot
continue to support ageing Australians without reviewing and altering the
country's revenue base (SuperGuide, 2014). Responsible alcohol management and the emerging issue of Australian mental health (a widely recognized boardroom issue) are key business social issues. In a transparent and
digital age, business is developing new brands, digital strategies and new
ways of connecting with consumers – but they have yet to associate the
digital world with resource scarcity or human rights issues.

The Australian environment is in distress. Given the agriculturally based
economy and a uniquely arid landscape, the need for businesses to manage
water, soil loss, salinity and acidity is ever increasing. Developing environmental resource extraction technologies, protecting the Great Barrier
Reef (the world's largest coral reef system), and responding to the threat of
climate change through emission reduction in transport and energy, are
key environmental priorities.

Trends

Few surveys focus on sustainable enterprise in Australia, and insights
about the CSR business sustainability priorities are patchy. The most
regular snapshot comes via the Australian Centre for Corporate Social
Responsibility (ACCSR)'s annual State of CSR survey (ACCSR, 2008–14).
The 2014 survey shows that CSR has "stalled" in Australia – with almost no
change over the past 12 months. Most are still preoccupied with "raising
awareness" (others feel current action is "insufficient"). It is worrying that
there is a lack of sustainability leadership by any sector in Australia. Most
large corporations are preoccupied with basic housekeeping issues, focused
on the "low hanging fruit" of responsiveness to regulatory demands,
promoting diversity in the workplace, and tightening supply chain policies.

Global surveys – particularly of Corporate Responsibility Reporting
produced by KPMG (KPMG, 1993–2013) – show that Australian companies

are becoming more strategic in how they approach CSR and sustaina-bility. Whether this represents a radical change to how companies are addressing the issues, or whether it shows "capture" of the agenda into existing business parlance is a moot point. The Australian Council of Superannuation Investors (ACSI) also lament the lack of responsiveness of the top 200 companies on sustainability issues and performance to stakeholders.

The picture is more encouraging for social enterprises. A 2010 study estimated that, of the more than 20,000 social enterprises in Australia (a 37% increase over the past five years), 73% had operated for longer than five years, and 62% for more than ten (Barraket *et al.*, 2010). The social enterprise sector is estimated to contribute 2–3% of GDP – equating to $22 billion (Barraket, Collyer, O'Connor, and Anderson, 2010). A 2011 University of New South Wales study of social entrepreneurs features 38 innovative social enterprises across the following sectors: food; arts, media and design; advocacy; information technology; environment; and services (Kernot and McNeill, 2011).

Government policies

Government policy focuses mostly on managing sustainability impacts, with no State or Federal policy on sustainable enterprise. Australian compa-nies are required to report under the National Greenhouse and Energy Reporting System (NGERS) if they have operational control of a facility that emits equal to or greater than a legal carbon/energy threshold (See Australian Government, Dept of Environment, 2014). Of consequence was the abolition and repealing of the Carbon Tax in July 2014, making Australia the first developed country to retrench its commitments to put a price on carbon, against the global trend of advancement in carbon reduction legis-lation and cap and trade schemes. This has wide-reaching implications for Australia as the world's 12th largest economy and one of the world's largest per capita greenhouse gas emitters (Taylor and Hoyle, 2014).

Information from reporting schemes are aggregated into five-yearly State of the Environment reports prepared for Government to monitor environ-mental trends, guide policy, consider major causal factors, and contribute to public education.

In 2013, Regulatory Guide 247 was introduced to company legislation requiring listed companies to disclose information about their strategies, prospects and material business risks (including from social and environmental issues) in an Operating and Financial Review in their annual report. The intent is to provide investors with a picture of a company's long-term prospects and quality of management (ASIC, 2013).

Many companies in the mining and extractive industries face regulatory processes associated with exploration and operations that require baseline audits of environmental characteristics, operational plans to minimize environmental impacts, stakeholder consultation, and remediation plans. These are typically administered by state-based environmental agencies and involve site-specific plans and conditions.

Unlike in certain states of the USA, Benefit Corporations (B Corps) are not yet recognized in Australia as legal corporate structures, but some changes are under way. The first Australian company to obtain the B Corp stamp was Small Giants – a private investment firm. Since its certification in July last 2012, around 15 others have followed, including the newly launched superfund Good Super.

Case studies

Bank MECU

Bank MECU, recognized in 2010 by Ethical Investor as Australia's most sustainable small company of the year, is a customer owned bank that has embraced innovative sustainability measures, including: The Conservation Landbank enabling Bank MECU to offset biodiversity loss and carbon emissions from financing new homes and cars, restoring endemic vegetation and protecting habitat on its properties. Further innovations include cards made from PETG environmentally responsible plastic and Bank Mecu's community resilience focus that addresses financial literacy, science and education development for teachers, and investing funds to prevent violence against women.

Desso

Carpet manufacturer Desso uses a cradle-to-cradle manufacturing process aimed at environmental restoration. Desso's breakthrough innovations include carpets that light up with LED powered information for emergency scenarios or fun patterns for a party. Desso has joined other carpet and apparel manufacturers in "Healthy Seas, a Journey from Waste to Wear" to take marine waste, particularly fishing nets, to create ECONYL (regenerated nylon yarn).

Just one of many of their designs is the Desso AirMaster® with EcoBase™ backing that was Highly Commended at the Australian Sustainability Awards for its health and wellbeing and environmental design values and that was also a finalist in the 2014 Australian BPN Sustainability Awards The AirMaster® is uniquely engineered to capture eight times more of the fine dust indoors than other flooring products. It comes with the EcoBase™, a polyolefin based backing (non-toxic and PVC-free) and achieved Cradle to Cradle® Silver Certification (with 100% of the materials being positively defined and 100% recyclable in Desso's production system). The DESSO AirMaster® carpet is also available with ECONYL® 100% regenerated yarn containing fishing net waste material from the Healthy Seas initiative (see above).

Lush

This beauty company "walks the talk" in all facets of business, from its Australian made, locally produced ethos, to its approach to packaging and waste and its charity pots. One product, Toothy Tabs, was a recent winner of the Australian Business Award for best Eco product 2013 and for environmental sustainability 2013. Toothy Tabs is a preservative-free solid toothpaste packaged in recycled and recyclable boxes. It was conceived in response to the waste associated with aluminium toothpaste tubes, and a desire to avoid excess packaging and preservatives. Toothy Tabs are crushed in the mouth to form a paste, then brushed like normal toothpaste. Their "charity pot" proceeds go towards local organizations.

Net Balance (EY)

In 2014, professional services firm EY Australia (formerly Ernst & Young) acquired Net Balance, Australia's leading dedicated sustainability consulting firm.

The combined EY and Net Balance team are the largest Australian sustainability service provider in the areas of sustainability strategy, reporting and assurance, social impact, carbon, energy, health, safety and environment.

The acquisition promises a blend of robust and innovative global management consulting balanced by the social impact approach of Net Balance to expand the firm's client base and offer deep technical expertise.

It also enables wider connections to more diverse businesses with unique expertise and the promise to take organizations to the next level of their sustainability journey.

Net Balance, previously an Australian B Corp, has had to renounce this B Corp status as part of the acquisition, but EY has retained the Net Balance Foundation, its non-profit arm.

YGAP

YGAP is a not-for-profit founded six years ago that uses partnerships to address global issues such as sex trafficking in Cambodia and education in Rwanda, as well as local Australian issues. YGAP uses creative fundraisers and social enterprise to support their projects. Their restaurant Feast of Merit in Melbourne uses local produce with all profits directed to YGAP's social outcomes. Their Australia-wide 5cent Campaign captures some of the $150 million of the five-cent coins in circulation for a good cause. Campaign innovations include sponsor organizations and individuals pledging 5¢ per dollar (i.e. 5% of their earnings) or 5¢ per product sold to YGAP. YGAP's projects model has evolved to focus on finding and enabling local social entrepreneurs in Africa and Australasia, helping them to scale their impact.

With an intention to truly make their mark, their recently released 2020 Vision document announced their goal of being 80% funded by social enterprise by 2020, plus a reported near tripling of earnings from 2013 to 2014, and the aim to reach 1 million people living in poverty. The future only promises to extend the innovation and impact YGAP's social enterprises will make.

Further resources

Australian Centre for Corporate Social Responsibility – A training and consulting centre, wholly dedicated to building competitive advantage and stakeholder wealth through corporate social responsibility.

Asia Pacific Centre for Sustainable Enterprise, Griffith University – Established to inform and assist the development of sustainable enterprise through innovative research, teaching and engagement activities.

Australian Centre for Sustainable Business Development (ACSBD) – Supports an applied research programme dedicated to promoting sustainable development through business and community sustainability innovations.

Australian Sustainable Business Group – ASBG is a business representative body helping organizations deal with the substantial and rapidly changing environmental, and greenhouse laws and helping them to become more sustainable.

Deakin University's Centre for Sustainable and Responsible Organizations (CSaRO) – CSaRO brings together researchers from a variety of disciplines to better understand and promote long-term sustainable and responsible organizational behaviour. The Centre undertakes thorough research and engages in dialogue with the research community, business leaders, policy advisers and the public at large.

Futureye – An international consultancy delivering social licence to operate solutions using insights and innovative approaches to provide specialist strategy, communications and engagement services to organizations facing public concerns about their operations.

Sustainable Business Australia – A business think-tank and advocacy group promoting commercial solutions to environmental challenges.

References

ACCSR (Australian Centre for Corporate Social Responsibility) (2008–14). The state of CSR. Melbourne: ACCSR.

ASIC (Australian Securities & Investment Commission) (2013). RG 247 Effective disclosure in an operating and financial review. Sydney: ASIC.

Australian Government (2011). Indigenous economic development strategy: 2011–2018. Canberra: Commonwealth of Australia.

Australian Government (Dept of Environment) (2014). Tracking Australia's greenhouse gas emissions. Canberra: Commonwealth of Australia.

Barraket, J., Collyer, N., O'Connor, M. & Anderson, H. (2010). Finding Australia's Social Enterprise Sector (FASES). Queensland: Australian Centre for Philanthropy and Non-Profit Studies.

Kernot, C. & McNeill, J. (2011). *Australian stories of social enterprise*. Sydney: University of New South Wales.

KPMG (1993–2013). The KPMG survey of corporate responsibility reporting. London: KPMG.

Taylor, R. & Hoyle, R. (2014, July 17). Australia becomes first developed nation to repeal carbon tax. *Asia: Wall Street Journal*, 160.

SuperGuide (2014). Age pension increasing to 70 years. 23 September.

2
Bangladesh

Md Nazmul Hasan
Doctoral Researcher, Royal Holloway, University of London, UK

Md Shafiqul Islam
Assistant Professor, University of Liberal Arts Bangladesh, Bangladesh

National context

Bangladesh is the youngest country of the South Asia region. With more than 160 million people living in 56,977 square miles, it is one of the most densely populated countries in the world. Bangladesh has made reasonable progress in reducing poverty, maintaining economic growth, achieving gender parity in education and eliminating famines and severe epidemics. Even so, due to its geographical position, Bangladesh is a disaster-prone low-lying country that faces serious environmental challenges, especially the effects of climate change.

A few multinational subsidiaries have plans for sustainability, but for most local enterprises in Bangladesh, the concept of sustainable and socially responsible business is still unknown. The textile (ready-made garments, or RMG) industry has been especially heavily criticized for poor occupational safety, bad working conditions and unsustainable production processes. The tragic Rana Plaza building collapse in 2013 brought many of these issues into focus in Bangladesh and around the world.

Priority issues

Despite strong economic growth (6.1% in 2013–14), Bangladesh's economy is hampered by political unrest, deteriorating relationships with key export markets and weak government policies on trade and industry. The country depends heavily on remittances from expatriate workers and export earnings, both of which are declining (Centre for Policy Dialogue, 2014) According to the latest data from the Central Bank of Bangladesh, remittance inflow decreased by more than 8% in the first half of 2014, compared with a 22% rise the previous year. Experts believe that this reduction is due to a decrease in the export of manpower, a lack of inclusive policies and ongoing political instability (New Age, 2014).

One major challenge for the current government is to win back the GSP (generalized system of preferences) to export duty-free products to the US market. This was removed by the Obama administration in 2013, citing serious shortcomings in safety standards and factory workers' rights, especially in the garment sector. This affects not only textiles, but also tobacco, sporting equipment, porcelain and plastic products. Other economic challenges for the government include raising tax revenues and curbing expenditure growth, as well as increasing domestic demand for home-produced products and developing new export markets.

Besides these social and economic issues, Bangladesh is one of the most affected victims of climate change, which exacerbates the tropical monsoon conditions with frequent floods, droughts, cyclones, river erosion and landslides, causing huge damage to lives and properties (UNESCO, 2012). Human and industrial activity also degrades the land, causing salinity, soil contamination, deforestation, water pollution and a falling water table (Bangladesh Ministry of Planning, 2013). Environmentally harmful industrial growth is especially prevalent in the tanning, textiles, shipbuilding, brick building and automotive sectors.

Trends

With the help of key development partners, international NGOs and local government (in some cases), sustainability is being applied to a variety of domestic industries. For instance, the SWITCH-Asia Programme, funded by the European Commission, is running a project to strengthen the export competitiveness of Bangladesh through promotion of environmentally friendly jute products. In 2012, the programme successfully completed another project that helped the Bangladeshi leather industry to reduce environmental impacts and increase the exportability of leather products.

Another example is the United Nations Development Programme (UNDP) five-year project for "Improving Kiln Efficiency in the Brick Making Industry". The project's aim is to remove barriers to the widespread adoption of energy-efficient kilns and energy efficiency practices for the brick-making industry in Bangladesh. A complementary project funded by the Asian Development Bank (ADB) is promoting market awareness and generating demand for funds to construct energy-efficient kilns.

The financial sector is also showing positive signs. For example, Bangladesh Bank adopted a green banking policy in 2011 and the government has recently provided aid to a local agency (with support from the World Bank) to devise a credit scheme for marketing solar home system units and making these an affordable alternative to grid electricity for poor people in remote areas (World Bank, 2013). On the other hand, a controversial political decision to build a large coal-fired power plant near the Sundarbans (the biggest mangrove forest in the world and a World Heritage Site) faced serious protests from environmentalists and local people throughout 2013.

Government policies

The most recent National Industrial Policy (2010) states that the government plans to provide incentives (tax and duty exemptions) to promote the adoption of environmentally sound manufacturing processes and practices. This includes providing facilities for waste recycling to encourage entrepreneurs to pursue the three "R"s (Reduce, Reuse and Recycle). The government has committed to support investment in projects designed to reduce the emission of greenhouse gases under the Kyoto Protocol's Clean Development Mechanism (CDM). Particular emphasis is also placed on the organic pesticide industry in order to protect the natural environment from the destruction of useful insects, soil microbes and aquatic life. Most recently, the government's ambitions have been captured in its 2013 National Sustainable Development Strategy (NSDS).

Case studies

Kazi Shahid Foundation

Kazi Shahid Foundation (KSF) was founded as a non-profit dairy cooperative to support KKTE. It is based on an innovative approach of providing beneficiaries with cows instead of cash. The cost of the cow is then repaid in milk and cow dung. Local people, especially women, are heavily involved in contract dairy farming, which could boost both their economic and their social status. KSF has seven branches where 1,060 members are engaged in contractual dairy farming. Two of these branches are now financed by Palli Karma Shahayak Foundation's LIFT project, which is expected to expand. Most of the beneficiaries of KSF cooperatives have now become entrepreneurs and started dairy cow rearing and selling milk and dung. Most of the members (particularly women) did not have any source of income before joining KSF, but now their income level has significantly increased from BDT 5,000 (approximately £40) to BDT 10,000 (approximately £80) per month.

mPower Social Enterprises Ltd

mPower Social Enterprises was founded with a view to leveraging the revolution in technology and mobile communications to help address development challenges. Harvard graduate Mridul Chowdhury, Rubayat Khan and their colleagues first tested their ideas in Africa, but given Chowdhury's ties to Bangladesh, in 2008 Click Diagnostics was started in Dhaka. The initiative was later renamed mPower Health, to reflect the company's expansion beyond remote diagnostics into holistic health systems management, before being given the even broader name of mPower Social Enterprises.

Clients are the many donors and NGOs operating in Bangladesh, which implement various development projects each year. For example, they have provided consultancy services to the Stimulating Household Improvements Resulting in Economic Empowerment (SHIREE) project, which is a partnership between the UK Department for International Development (DFID) and the Government of Bangladesh (GoB) to combat extreme poverty. With nearly a million programme beneficiaries throughout the country, serviced by over 40 implementing partner NGOs, monitoring partners and tracking progress is extremely difficult.

By 2013 the company had grown and begun to make a profit, although it inevitably experienced some growing pains. Chowdhury and his colleagues had to adapt to the demands of a larger company, and to generate solutions to different types of problem.

Pabna Meat

The idea of Pabna Meat was conceived by Md. Liaquat Ali, a director of Bengal Meat, the largest meat processing company in Bangladesh. He envisioned an entirely vertically integrated business producing quality organic meat for the end-consumer. The business model allows rural women to rear cattle by feeding them organic food and then sell the fattened cattle to the company as a source of income. It is a potential win–win scenario: Pabna Meat obtains the cattle it needs, and the women improve their standard of living.

Among the obstacles faced were low income levels among rural women, who did not have the money to purchase and rear cattle, and inadequate training. Ali's solution was to put together a four-way collaboration between Pabna Meat, the Business Innovation Facility (BIF), a group promoting inclusive businesses, Practical Action Bangladesh, a national NGO working with rural women, and Bangladesh Association for Social Advancement (BASA), a listed microfinance institution in Bangladesh. Pabna Meat is now supplying processed meat and meat products in a number of five star hotels and high-end restaurants within the capital.

Teatulia

Kazi & Kazi Tea Estate Limited (KKTE) is a 1,400-acre organic tea plantation in north-western Bangladesh. Founded in 2000, by 2013 KKTE was producing over 300,000 kg of tea, 50,000 kg of which were being sold under the brand name Teatulia, the first branded Bangladeshi tea in the US market. Teatulia is grown using sustainable agricultural practices, and it commands a premium price in recognition of its quality. The lives of many people in the KKTE areas have improved noticeably, as has the local economy.

Many local farmers grow their own tea, and over 2,200 people, mostly women, are employed in the tea plantation and its vegetable, herb and dairy operations. They are paid market-rate wages on time, unlike many wage earners in the region. Workers receive training in organic cultivation and also in composting, mulching and pest management. Local people also benefit indirectly by supplying sand, topsoil, stone, dairy feed, bamboo and other materials used in the tea plantation and its dairy and vegetable operations. KKTE has helped local people to build hundreds of safe latrines, conducted health and hygiene programmes, and distributed sports equipment to local people.

Further resources

GIZ (German Society for International Cooperation) – Has been helping Bangladesh on a number of sustainable development projects since 1972.

Katalyst – A private-sector development project that aims to contribute to sustainable economic development both in rural and urban areas of Bangladesh.

Reed Consulting (Bangladesh) Ltd – An international consulting firm working on private-sector development in Bangladesh since 2006.

References

Bangladesh Ministry of Planning (2013). National sustainable development strategy (NSDS). Dhaka: Government of Bangladesh.

Centre for Policy Dialogue (CPD) (2014). Analytical review of Bangladesh's macro-economic performance in FY2014 (second reading). Dhaka: CPD.

New Age (2014) Remittance inflow drops after 14 yrs. 4 July.

UNESCO (United Nations Educational, Scientific and Cultural Organization) (2012). UNESCO country programming document for Bangladesh 2012–2016. Paris: UNESCO.

World Bank (2013). Implementation Completion and Results Report. Rural Electrification and Renewable Energy Development Project. Washington, DC.: World Bank.

Acknowledgements

The Pabna Meat case was originally prepared by Shubhankar Shil and Nazmul Hasan as part of the Bangladesh Business Case Study Writing Project, which was initiated by the University of Liberal Arts Bangladesh (ULAB) in July 2012.

We are grateful to David Bowker, Teaching Fellow, School of Education, University of Stirling (Scotland), for his useful comments and suggestions on the first draft of this chapter.

3
Cambodia

Muneezay Jaffery
Operations Manager, Green Shoots Foundation, UK

Akash Ghai
Co-Founder, Development Three, USA

National context

According to 2007 World Bank data (Knowles, 2009), poverty rates in Cambodia were around 30%, with 77% of Cambodians living in rural areas, of which 34.5% live below the poverty line. It is difficult to present population estimates as the last national census was conducted in 1998 and excluded areas in the north, which were a Khmer Rouge stronghold. Cambodia has had a tumultuous recent history of violence and destruction that has impacted the country's sociopolitical environment and economic growth.

On a national scale, the Khmer Rouge-led genocide and 30 years of civil war have left severe gaps in the population pyramid, with middle-aged populations (particularly male) missing. This has resulted in a high dependence ratio of an ageing population coupled with the emergence of an increasingly youthful population. The latter can be advantageous to the country, provided policies that support youth are in place. It is important to note that during the Khmer Rouge regime (1975–79), extensive infrastructure was destroyed, small enterprises were forbidden and trade, markets and money were banned. The Khmer Rouge enforced "absolute self-sufficiency", which resulted in famine and illness-related deaths, as medicine and basic healthcare were depleted.

After 1979 Cambodia embarked on nearly a decade of civil unrest, sporadic fighting in rural areas and an extensive influx of assistance from the international community. Geographically, Cambodia nestles between Thailand, Laos and Vietnam, countries that have offered assistance in times of conflict and also encourage cross-border trade. However, Thailand and Vietnam also offer better employment prospects and wage earners living near the border towns often choose to emigrate and take on low-skilled work.

Priority issues

Cambodia is predominately an agricultural based economy with agri-food activity accounting for 72% of national employment in 2008 (Maclean *et al.*, 2012). Yet it generates only 32% of the total GDP, as most farming is subsistence based.

In the last two decades Cambodia has begun to achieve high economic growth, predominantly led by the garment industry and trade links with China. The government exhibits a focus on the manufacturing industry and the setting up of Special Economic Zones, creating dependence on foreign investment. The lack of diversity in the economy makes Cambodia socio-economically vulnerable, with bouts of migration and a growing disconnect between urban and rural areas. This also means social services such as healthcare, education and access to finance perform poorly in Cambodia and are left to the non-profit sector.

The lure of urban areas is resulting in a decline in rural populations and consequently also in agricultural activity. Recent flooding episodes and dry spells, resulting in a poor harvest, together with environmental degradation due to over-use of chemicals and poor water management, reinforces the urbanization trend. As many of these migrants lack appropriate skills, education and professional experience for the urban labour market, they rely on informal trade.

According to the ILO (2014), the informal economy in Cambodia – including street vendors selling food, services providers such as barbers, tailors or taxi drivers, and subsistence farmers – accounted for 62% of GDP and 85% of the total workforce. Lyne (2012) states that researchers tend to conflate the informal economy with the "social entrepreneurship economy" (Lyne, 2012).

Trends

Conceptually, sustainable enterprise and assisting communities is not rare in Cambodia due its abject poverty and the influx of aid in the 1990s. Nonetheless, most practitioners recognize an urgent need for catalysing and legitimizing the sustainable entrepreneurship sector, in order to empower local populations and move away from corrupt governments and reliance on international aid agencies and NGOs. It is widely recognized that these charitable approaches have a poor and outdated understanding of local needs.

Increasingly, the technical expertise for developing the sustainable enterprise sector is being introduced by international NGOs and expatriates living in Cambodia. These organizations can be described as having "commercial activities with a social purpose" and many are working towards preserving and promoting artisanal skills that were disintegrated by the Khmer Rouge. This approach has been the most successful as it ties in neatly with Cambodia's burgeoning tourism industry.

The Cambodian sustainable enterprise market is essentially filling gaps where the government is failing, making it a niche activity. Although workshops for social and sustainable enterprises are common in urban areas, at $10 per session, they remain inaccessible to the vast majority. According to Hutchinson and Molla (2009), the growth of sustainable enterprises is constrained by the availability of technology such as computers and the internet, and gaps in ICT skills.

Government policies

According to Social Enterprise Cambodia (Pour un Sourire d'Enfant Cambodia, 2014), there is still no legislation on social or sustainable enterprise. "It's been talked about for a while but nothing is likely to come in." At the moment, most sustainable enterprises are either registered as non-profit organizations or as small businesses. NGOs pursuing business activities operate in a legal vacuum. The recommended solution is obtaining commercial status as a sole trader or a small and medium-sized enterprise (SME), thus allowing them to distribute dividends plus accept investment and shareholders.

A recent ILO (2014) report suggests a change in the government's approach to achieving SME growth. New legislation has been introduced to streamline and reduce registration procedures and lower the capital required to register a SME. The government is eager to encourage entre-preneurial prowess among youth and individual entrepreneurs. Non-profit organizations operating in Cambodia also often highlight small-scale efforts of individuals in the creation of value.

Case studies

Banteay Chhmar

Banteay Chhmar is the eponymous village in north Cambodia, named after the 12th century Angkor Temple located there. In 2006 it was renovated by the Global Heritage Fund and earmarked for a Community Based Tourism (CBT) venture. A CBT incorporates the entire community in tourism activ-ities through home-stay options, local restaurants and other businesses. This is an ideal sustainable enterprise as it enhances local livelihoods and has positive social, economic and environmental impacts.

A typical trip can involve: Exploring the historical site with a local guide, eating food prepared at a restaurant or a picnic prepared by the local women, spending a night in a traditional wooden home and visiting the Mekong Silk centre (Tourism Cambodia, 2014). An added environmental feature is that most of the homes have solar panels installed. One drawback is the remoteness of the village and poor transport links to the complex. Other CBT examples in Cambodia tend to focus either on ecology or wildlife but have proved less successful as they require better maintenance and upkeep.

Cambodian Centre for Study and Development in Agriculture (CEDAC)

CEDAC is an enterprise working on sustainable agriculture in rural areas by facilitating the organization of farm cooperatives, and teaching them how to lower resource inputs and improve crop yields. Taught techniques include better water management using drip irrigation and growing all year round through mixed cropping. To ensure maximum outreach, CEDAC partner with other local charities for training delivery, publish a farmers' magazine and operate a radio station. Partnering with local charities allows them to subsidize the cost of farming equipment such as irrigation systems and drum seeders. CEDAC is currently registered as a non-profit organization and started out in 1997 with only seven employees. It now employs over 220 people and directly impacts the lives of 160,000 people in 22 provinces of Cambodia.

International Development Enterprises (iDE) Cambodia

iDE is an international NGO that has been active in Cambodia since 1994, working primarily in the water and sanitation sector. It is typical of the kinds of sustainable enterprise that are filling in gaps where government is failing. In 2001, with initial funding from a UK grant-maker, they established a commercial subsidiary, Hydrologic, to sell ceramic water filters in Cambodia. The grant money was used to set up a factory and manufacture ceramic pots that are able to filter water. iDE also recruited and trained local agents from rural villages to spread awareness about clean water and sanitation.

To date, the filters have been used extensively by non-profit organizations and sold through microfinance institutions (MFIs), making the technology accessible and affordable. The filter uses local materials during construction and has environmental benefits, as it reduces the need for cutting and burning wood fuel to boil water. The economic and social benefits of this approach are in fuel spending savings, noticeable health-related improvements and the provision of employment in factories and for village agents.

PEPY Cambodia

Another, more mainstream, example of a sustainable enterprise in the tourism and hospitality industry is PEPY – Promoting Education, emPowering Youth. This is an NGO that supports education in Cambodian villages with a strong focus on youth empowerment. PEPY is registered as a non-profit organization in the USA and they also operate a commercial enterprise, PEPY Tours, which is registered as a sustainable tourism company. The founder of PEPY owns the enterprise (Tours) and a board of seven members governs the NGO.

PEPY Tours provides bespoke adventures and experiences around Cambodia allowing participants to learn about responsible tourism and

Khmer culture. They contribute financial support to the work of PEPY Cambodia, which includes their schools located in two provinces of Cambodia. The sustainable enterprise model that PEPY employs began as a fundraising initiative by four friends for a one-off cycling adventure across Cambodia, while learning and contributing to education programmes in the region. Its success was replicated and scaled up as a business model to continue sustaining the non-profit activities.

Soieries du Mékong

Soieries du Mékong was established by Enfants du Mékong (EDM), a French charity operating in South-East Asia since the 1950s. EDM has set up education centres and boarding houses for youth to pursue formal education or vocational training in rural and urban areas. EDM is the majority shareholder of Soieries du Mékong and together they secure the livelihoods of Cambodians, particularly women, and promote fair-trade and eco-fashion in France and online. Soieries du Mekong was set up to combat migration of unskilled Cambodians to the cities of Thailand by providing training on how to weave silk, manufacture scarves and secure individuals' long-term economic development.

In the absence of policies or regulations for social enterprises in Cambodia, Soieries du Mékong follows its own Ethical Charter, which commits to providing the weavers with work all year round, paying fair wages, offering basic financial management training, covering medical expenses and organizing a savings plan. The Soieries du Mekong training facilities and workshop are based within the Banteay Chhmar complex.

Further resources

Social Enterprise Cambodia – An independent initiative dedicated to promoting social entrepreneurship in the Kingdom. This is a place for established social enterprises to connect and grow and for new start-ups to learn more about the sector. They provide a platform for social entrepreneurs operating in Cambodia to share experiences, resources and ideas.

References

Hutchinson, K. & Molla, A. (2009). Mapping the dynamics of social enterprises and ICTD in Cambodia. IEEE/ACM International Conference on ICTD2009, 17–19 April 2009, Doha, Qatar.

ILO (2014). The Enabling Environment for Sustainable Enterprises in Cambodia. Geneva: International Labour Organization.

Knowles, J.C. (2009). Poverty profile and trend in Cambodia: Findings from the 2007 Cambodia Socio-Economic Survey (CSES). Washington, DC: World Bank.

Lyne, I. (2012). Social enterprise and social entrepreneurship as models of sustainability for local NGOs: learning from Cambodia. *International Journal for Management Research*, 2(1), 1-6.

Maclean, R., Jagannathan, S., & Sarvi, J. (2012). Skills development for inclusive and sustainable growth in developing Asia-Pacific. Technical and Vocational Education and Training: Issues, Concerns and Prospects, Vol. 19

Pour un Sourire d'Enfant Cambodia (2014). Survey on social business in Cambodia. Report by A. Tigé. Versailles.

Tourism Cambodia (2014). Banteay Chhmar community-based tourism site. Phnom Penh: Government of Cambodia.

4
China

Shuyi Zhang
Professor of Innovation and Entrepreneurship, Shanghai Finance University, China

National context

In 1978 the Chinese government initiated economic reforms and an open policy for trade and investment, which stimulated market demand, entrepreneurial activity and access to advanced technology. With multinational companies entering domestic markets and local firms investing abroad, China's economic growth increased rapidly over the ensuing three decades. Today, China ranks as the second largest economy in the world, with a population of 1.36 billion and GDP per capita of US$6,800.

Although China's economic achievement have been dramatic, it has been at the expense of the environment, as a result of following the traditional Western development model of high resource input, high consumption, high pollution and low efficiency. This problem is evident from high levels of city haze (smog), heavy metal pollution, chemical contamination and persistent organic pollutants. This has led to associated social problems, such as health impacts.

In response to these challenges, the new Chinese political leadership is emphasizing a clean environment to complement the country's political, cultural and social development, with the aim of building harmony and a sustainable society.

Priority issues

After the economic boom of the last three decades the Chinese government is targeting 7.5% GDP annual growth. The aim is to transform the country's economic model and economic structure by no longer using short-term stimulus policies to tackle temporary fluctuations. This will allow the market to play a critical role, which is one of the most important decisions made by the third plenary session of the 18th meeting of the Communist Party of China (CPC).

Since Xi Jinping took power in 2012, the new leadership has put forward eight rules to crack down on ever-spreading corruption, including increased discipline, criticizing dishonourable behaviour, and prosecuting criminal cases to correct formism and bureaucracy, hedonism and extravagance. Up to the end of September 2014, more than 137,000 executive examination and approval cases were exempted from traditional governmental departments, and more than 53 billion yuan of public spending used on going abroad, purchasing cars and official receptions was reduced. Many CPC members were investigated or punished for wrong doing, including 4,144 for participating in banquets or recreational activities using public funds, 2,550 for accepting bribe envelopes or shopping cards, and 7,162 for engaging in gambling, for instance. The public opinion polls show that nearly 90% of the people believe that these policies are working.

China is struggling to deal with the costs of environmental degradation, including impacts on air, water and food. The heavy haze is a result of air pollution, while worsening water shortages and water pollution pose a growing threat to economic and social development. Contaminated food also is also discovered periodically.

Trends

According to the "Survey Report of China Remarkable Enterprises on Sustainable Development" released by Sohu and ATKearney in 2011 (ATKearney, 2011), all companies applying for public appraisal participating have established their sustainable development strategy, among which, 83% have a written strategy, 83% issued a sustainable development strategy annually, and 95% implemented their strategy through the board of directors. Regarding ecological and societal dimensions, all participants paid much attention to ecological developments from various aspects. Sixty-seven per cent have put their plan into practice with effective results, especially in the fields of carbon emissions, water and renewable resources.

In a recent Climatescope report (issued on 28 October 2014) (Bloomberg, 2014) that provides data and analysis about clean energy investment covering 55 developing countries in Asia, Africa, Latin America and the Caribbean, claimed that the China investment index of clean energy is the highest among developing countries. Actually, China recognizes that energy security and the stability of energy supplies are the foundation of its economic security, Chinese government has made clean technology expansion a foundation of its energy security and economic development plans and has taken many actions to address this problem For instance, China has planned to invest $740 billion in the cleantech sector by 2020 (Chapman and Qian, 2012).

Regarding sustainable development, NGOs, especially the social enterprise, play a key role in China. There are two kinds of NGO organization: one has a top-down structure with a long history and supported partially by the government; the others are established by non-governmental figures, and typically focus on environmental protection, poverty relief and women's issues.

The Society of Entrepreneurs and Ecology (SEE), one of the most famous NGOs in China, was founded in 2004 by Shi Wang, the Chairman of Vanke, one of the largest real estate companies in China, together with about 60 other businessmen. The mission is to promote awareness and action on climate change and other environmental issues in Alashan, a desert located in Inner Mongolia, China. With the help of more than 300 members and numerous volunteers, SEE has implemented a programme including desert surveys, vegetation protection, groundwater protection, education and public participation, community development, etc. More than 200 million RMB Yuan has been invested to improve and restore the ecological environment, so as to slow down and curb sand storms.

Government policies

Following the UN's Earth Summit in Rio de Janeiro in 1992, the Chinese government adopted Agenda 21 and a series of regulations and rules covering population and family planning, environmental protection, natural resources and energy saving.

The 12th five-year programme for the national economy and social development (2011–15) pays particular attention to fighting climate change through low-carbon development. The state council has a work programme to control greenhouse gas emissions and goals for 2015. China's 2011 white paper on climate change policies and action addressed seven key areas, including adjusting the industrial structure, energy conservation, optimizing the energy mix and increasing carbon sinks.

The revised Environmental Protection Act (2014) will take effect on 1 January 2015 with the aim of waging war on pollution and seriously punishing those who discharge pollutants without efficient disposal.

At a regional level, nearly every provincial or local government has announced their emission reduction plans with annual goals. Some big cities such as Shanghai, Beijing and Hang Zhou have instituted a bidding or lottery system for getting car licence plates in order to control the number of cars and hence lower pollution levels. Another measure taken by local government is to initiate the carbon emission trading markets; seven local carbon exchanges have been established in Beijing, Shanghai, Guangdong, Tianjin, etc., with the total volume estimated to surpass 24 million tonnes in 2014 and 227 million tonnes in 2015. Chinese government initiatives to regulate the carbon exchange in fact aim at establishing national carbon exchange in the next three years.

Keeping pace with resource conservation and low-carbon trends, the Chinese government has enacted a series of regulations encouraging technology innovation, low carbon emissions and social responsibility, which are also reflected in national sustainable development strategies. For example, there are policies to decrease carbon emissions by 40–50% against a 2005 baseline and requirements for provincial governments to lower GDP energy consumption and carbon dioxide concentration by 16–17% by the end of 2020. The central government will evaluate the performance of provincial governments and publish it for public review. On 15 May 2014, China released The Action Plan of Energy Consumption, Emissions Reduction and Low Carbon Development (2014–15), to help fulfil the obligatory target for saving energy and reducing pollutant emissions according to the 12th five-year plan.

Case studies

APP-China

Asia Pulp & Paper (APP) is one of the top ten largest pulp and paper companies in the world founded by the famous Chinese Indonesian Huang Yicong. APP-China has focused on operations in the Yangtze River and Pearl River Delta since 1992, and has invested in several large world-leading pulp and paper companies. Following the sustainable economic model of plantation–pulp–paper integration, all the pulp and paper companies under APP-China have passed ISO 14001 international environment certification. Moreover, 17 companies have earned the Chain of Custody Certificate from the Programme for the Endorsement of Forest Certification.

As a leader in the global pulp and paper industry, APP recognizes that a sustainable paper industry is attainable only by managing conflicts surrounding growing market demand, environmental concerns and the lack of resources. In line with this, it published an upgraded manifesto in August 2011, which outlines the company's sustainability pledges and objectives, to realize an equal balance of the three pillars of sustainability that encompass economic, social and environmental development. In the past few years, APP-China strictly followed its commitments throughout its operations and continuously progressed in the three key areas of sustainable plantation, clean production and corporate social responsibility.

By the end of 2012, APP-China had planted over 300,000 ha of plantations on government approved degraded, waste or low value lands, which not only provides raw materials for paper production, but also benefits the environment and local farmers. Also, it spent over $1 billion on environmental protection facilities and $105 million on various charitable causes and community development projects across the country.

Beijing Shenwu Environment & Energy Technology Co., Ltd

Shenwu Corporation provides energy solutions to ensure highly efficient and clean utilization of fossil and mineral resources, environmental protection and atmospheric haze control. With 127 patents granted at home and abroad, it has established a series of national and industrial standards for energy savings and emissions reductions covering eight new technology areas, such as regenerative high-efficiency, energy-saving and low-pollution combustion and regenerative gasification boilers for low grade pulverized coal. It has invested RMB 500 million Yuan to build the only laboratory in China equipped with 18 large-scale pilot-test platforms, which enables it to conduct innovative research in the areas of fossil resources, mineral resources and renewable resources, and a self-contained manufacturing base with an investment of RMB 400 million Yuan to manufacture key energy-saving components.

China Recycling Development Co., Ltd

Established in 1989, China Recycling Development Corporation is the leading and largest resource recycling company in China. Focusing on waste steel, ferrous metal, paper, plastics, house appliances, scrap cars, etc., it has more than 50 branches or subsidiaries, with 3,000 recycling stations, five recycling demonstration bases and a capacity of recycling 10 million tonnes annually. Collaborating with universities and the academic community, it has also conducted recycling technology research based at its Tianjin recycling resources institute, national recycling information centre, and specific skill appraisal station.

Proctor & Gamble (P&G)

P&G is a publicly traded company, which serves approximately 4.8 billion people around the world. Since its entry into China in 1988, P&G (China) has committed to sustainable development through sustainable innovation of its products and responsible management of its supply chain. This is in line with its corporate motto of "touching lives, improving life".

P&G (China) has a programme called Greenovation, through which it not only reduces the use of energy, water and raw materials, but also improves economic and social development. The company's goal is to use 100% renewable energy and 100% sustainable sourced, renewable or recycled materials in all their products and packaging. From the beginning of 2010, the energy consumption per unit of production decreased by 8%, carbon emissions decreased by 11%; the ratio of cold washing water to total water washed by machine was 38% in 2010 and 50% in 2011; the renewable resource utilization level climbed to 7.5%, the transportation distance per unit of production decreased roughly 12% since 2010, and waste material out of the total raw materials has been 0.65% since 2010. Now, it has set a 2020 goal of obtaining 30% of its energy from renewable sources and two recent projects, Huangpu Solar and Taicang Wing, are rapidly developing.

P&G's corporate volunteer programme involves 70,000 hours from 5,000 volunteers who help 50,000 people under the theme of "life, study and growth". It has also established 200 Hope primary schools that benefit 5,000 more students and donates products and time to help with disaster relief efforts after earthquakes and floods.

Tsingtao Beer

Tsingtao Beer draws on the strength of its brand; finances and technology support a leading national R&D platform, which spawns technology innovation. This has resulted in super-high-end brewing techniques and rapid fermentation technology, which are all internationally leading examples of green technology.

In accordance with the environmental philosophy of "good mind, good find", the company has invested RMB470 million in energy efficiency and environmental protection projects. This has resulted in pollutant emissions compliance of 100% and reductions in pollutants (chemical oxygen demand and sulphur dioxide), water and coal. By applying recycling technology, carbon dioxide in the fermentation process is collected and reuse in the filling process, thereby reducing greenhouse gas emissions and saving costs.

Tsingtao Beer's occupational health and safety management systems ensured no human casualties in 2013. Employees pay increased 15.6% in 2013 and the average training time was 18.89 hours. It also donated RMB12 million and volunteers to help earthquake victims.

Further resources

Boao Forum for Asia – A non-governmental and non-profit international organization that organizes a popular annual conference that acts as a high-end dialogue platform for government officials, enterprises, experts and academics to discuss economic, social and environmental issues.

Chinese Society for Sustainable Development – A national academic social organization comprising of experts, scholars, and entrepreneurs who are concerned about issues regarding sustainable development.

China Sustainable Development Study – Initiated and organized by the Chinese Academy of Science and is in charge of compiling and publishing the China Sustainable Development Report annually.

References

ATKearney (2011). Survey report of China remarkable enterprises on sustainable development 2011. Chicago.

Bloomberg, (2014). Climatescope 2014 – Global study shows clean energy activity surges in developing world. Bloomberg New Energy Finance, 28 October.

Chapman, L.L. & Qian, W. (2012). Clean technology innovation in China: trends and challenges. Lexology, 13 February.

Sustainable Development Research Group of Chinese Academy of Science (2013). China sustainable development report 2013: the road to ecological civilization: next decade (in Chinese). Beijing: Science Press.

5
India

Karina Yadav
Founder, CSRway, India

Aparna Mahajan
Director, Resource Mobilization and Partnerships, S M Sehgal Foundation, India

National context

India, the world's second most populous country and second fastest growing major economy, has witnessed unprecedented development since economic liberalization in 1990s. Since independence, there has been phenomenal change. The country has become a global agricultural powerhouse, life expectancy has more than doubled, literacy rates have quadrupled, health conditions have improved and there is a burgeoning middle class.

By 2020, India is set to become world's youngest country with almost 64% of its population of working age. Enhancing workforce productivity could see India capturing significant benefits from this demographic dividend. However, the nation continues to face numerous development challenges, most notably poverty and climate change. It is likely that civil society – with one NGO for every 400 people in the country – will become even more important.

The goal of sustainability is prompting the emergence of many innovative businesses and social entrepreneurs (WWF and CII-ITC Centre of Excellence for Sustainable Development, 2008). According to a report on

"Insights from CEOs in the Global Compact Network India" (UN Global Compact and Accenture, 2013), two-thirds of CEOs of Indian companies believe that sustainability is very important to the future success of their business, although less than half (44%) think that business is making sufficient efforts in this direction.

Priority issues

In spite of India being the third-largest economic power by purchasing power parity (PPP) after the USA and China, the country is facing major developmental challenges. Critical issues include high unemployment, poverty, income disparity, corruption and inadequate education, health and nutrition. Moreover, despite a rich natural environment where just 2.4% of the world's land area accounts for approximately 7% of globally recorded species, India is grappling with pollution, climate change, environmental degradation and resource depletion.

India is one of the lowest "medium development" countries, ranked 136th on the 2013 UN Human Development Index. In order to lift 270 million people (22% of the population) out of extreme poverty, the country will have to tackle the scourge of corruption, as India is consistently placed among the most corrupt countries in Transparency International's Corruption Perceptions Index.

Rapid economic growth post-liberalization in 1990s, along with an increasing population, has caused severe environmental impacts, especially linked to water and resource scarcity, along with global climate change. The World Bank (2013) estimates that environmental degradation costs India $80 billion per year, or 5.7% of its GDP. Green growth is an obvious solution, paving the way to a low-emission, resource efficient economy.

Trends

While social initiatives, community development and CSR are part and parcel of many businesses, a more holistic approach – where sustainability and responsibility are embedded in the strategy, operations and products of companies – is the exception rather than the rule in India. Today's business strategies are largely driven by cost and risk reduction, along with reputation and legitimacy concerns, whereas sustainable value creation driven by innovation and growth is yet to mainstream. Nevertheless, India's social enterprise sector in growing, demonstrating the creativity and enthusiasm of the nation.

The social enterprise space in India is diverse, ranging across numerous sectors, from agriculture, energy, water and sanitation to education, healthcare and financial services (Asian Development Bank, 2012). These ventures are mostly immature, with nearly half of social enterprises being in existence for less than two years, as revealed in "On the Path to Sustainability and Scale: A Study of India's Social Enterprise Landscape" by Intellecap (2012) in 2012. Fabindia, SELCO Solar and Grameen Financial Services are some of the more time tested success stories that have transformed the lives of many of India's less fortunate.

Looking to the future, with 2010–20 announced as the "decade of innovations" by the Government of India, sustainable and inclusive enterprises are likely to form an important part of the business response to India's socioeconomic and environmental challenges (CII-ITC Centre of Excellence for Sustainable Development, 2010). Sanitation is set to become one of the key intervention areas as a national-level campaign, Swachh Bharat (Clean India), was launched by Prime Minister Narenda Modi in 2014.

Government policies

To promote inclusive and sustainable development, the Government of India has taken an active role in institutionalizing sustainable and responsible business practices, both through mandatory and voluntary means.

In 2009, the Ministry of Corporate Affairs released the Corporate Governance Voluntary Guidelines and the Corporate Social Responsibility Voluntary Guidelines, with the latter being upgraded to the National Voluntary Guidelines on Social, Environmental and Economic Responsibilities of Business in 2011. The Department of Public Enterprise also introduced CSR policies for 249 central public-sector enterprises (CPSE) in 2010, to counterbalance the profit and shareholder focus that market liberalization had brought.

The most recent game-changing mandate is part of the new Companies Act 2013, which obliges organizations of a certain strength to allocate 2% of their net profits to CSR. This law is expected to cover approximately 6,000 companies and to cause an estimated INR27,000 crore (approximately US$4.4 billion) to flow into grass-roots development and social enterprise sectors every year. The Act also makes CSR a board-level responsibility with reporting on CSR being part of a board's annual report (KPMG, 2013). The limitation to this legislation is that it restricts CSR to activities that are not part of the core business.

Case studies

Hindustan Unilever Limited (HUL): Project Shakti

Hindustan Unilever is India's largest FMCG company, touching the lives of two out of three Indians. Project Shakti is a rural distribution and micro-enterprise initiative by the company that promotes livelihoods in small villages and improves access to quality products in rural India. The Shakti model is strong, sustainable and scalable. It not only extends Hindustan Unilever's market share in rural areas, but it also creates livelihood opportunities for underprivileged rural women.

Shakti started with 17 women in one state and, today, it provides livelihood enhancing opportunities to 48,000 women in 15 Indian states, with access to quality products across 100,000+ villages and over 3 million households every month. Project Shakti has provided business opportunities to the male members of the family too, who can service outlets not only in their own village but also in nearby villages. The project is being customized and adapted in several South-East Asian, African and Latin American markets.

Fabindia

Fabindia is an urban handicraft retail chain that was founded in 1960 and is regarded as India's oldest social enterprise. Its production network comprises over 80,000 craft-based rural artisans who are organized into producer groups, operating as NGOs, social enterprises or community owned companies (COC).

The unique COC model, actively promoted by Fabindia since 2007, upholds the idea of inclusive capitalism. By providing at least 26% shareholding in COCs to the artisans, Fabindia is not only offering regular incomes to rural craft-persons but also shares the dividends from company's growth with them.

The retail chain has risen from a small outlet in New Delhi to more than 170 stores across India and abroad. Besides enabling skilled and sustainable rural employment, Fabindia serves as a platform for traditional crafts and knowledge, preserving long-standing culture and traditions.

Pollinate Energy

Pollinate Energy has established a microdistribution network for appropriate and affordable green household products, targeting urban poor migrant communities in the slums of Bangalore that rely on kerosene for their daily lighting requirements. Their mission is to create job opportunities for local entrepreneurs (who they call Pollinators) to start their own businesses as microdistributors that bring clean energy technology, in the form of small-scale solar lights, directly to the most needy communities.

Pollinate Energy trains local people in technical and entrepreneurial skills and supports them as they build clean energy micro-franchises. These franchises service urban slum residents with clean energy products, such as solar systems and smokeless cooking stoves. Pollinate Energy's clean energy solutions help fight widespread energy poverty by effectively reaching out to the increasing numbers of urban slum communities, both as customers and distributors.

Sustaintech India

Sustaintech India is a social enterprise, which starting its operations in Tamil Nadu in 2011. It distributes a line of environmentally friendly, fuel-efficient commercial cooking stoves, targeting street food vendors and commercial kitchens. The company is extending sustainable energy technologies to lower-income communities, creating positive financial, environmental and health impacts, and promoting climate change adaptation. They have consciously made the decision to adopt a for-profit social enterprise model. By selling its products, not only is Sustaintech generating profits but also positive social and environmental impacts. Sustaintech India won the United Nations Environment Programme (UNEP) 2013 SEED Low Carbon Award.

SELCO Solar

SELCO Solar, a social enterprise established in 1995, provides sustainable energy solutions and services to under-served households and businesses. SELCO has brought solar lighting systems to more than 125,000 rural households with limited or no access to electricity. It was conceived in an effort to dispel myths associated with sustainable technology and the rural sector as a target customer base, that poor people cannot afford and maintain sustainable technologies, and that social ventures cannot be run as commercial entities.

SELCO aims to empower its customers by providing a complete package of product, service and consumer financing through Grameen banks, cooperative societies, commercial banks and microfinance institutions. Through provision of solar lights, SELCO has been able to successfully empower individuals to run their businesses without dependence on fuel-based products for lighting. Its mission is to seed and mentor similar ventures in the sustainable energy space through the SELCO Incubation Center.

Further resources

CII-ITC Centre of Excellence for Sustainable Development – The CII-ITC Centre supports government and business in tackling sustainability issues and aims to be the guiding force behind the transition to a sustainable economy.

India Council for Sustainable Development – ICSD is an NGO that provides guidance and relevant analysis on integrating environmental concerns with development, laying specific emphasis on poverty alleviation and ensuring equitable growth of income and wealth in India.

New Ventures India – This joint partnership between the Confederation of Indian Industry, Godrej Green Business Centre and the World Resources Institute helps sustainable business entrepreneurs overcome business challenges and achieve environmental improvement in India.

TERI Business Council for Sustainable Development – TERI-BCSD is an independent, credible platform for corporate leaders to address issues related to sustainable development and promote leadership in environmental management, social responsibility and economic performance.

References

Asian Development Bank (2012). India social enterprise landscape report. Mandaluyon: Asian Development Bank.

CII-ITC Centre of Excellence for Sustainable Development (2010). Sustainable & inclusive innovation: strategies for tomorrow's world. New Delhi: CII-ITC CESD.

Intellecap (2012). On the path to sustainability and scale: a study of India's social enterprise landscape. Mumbai: Intellecap.

KPMG (2013). India corporate responsibility reporting survey 2013. Mumbai: KPMG.

UN Global Compact & Accenture (2013). CEO Study on Sustainability. New York.

World Bank (2013). India: Diagnostic Assessment of Select Environmental Challenges – An Analysis of Physical and Monetary Losses of Environmental Health and Natural Resources. Volume 1. Agriculture and Rural Development Sector Unit: Washington, DC.

WWF and CII-ITC Centre of Excellence for Sustainable Development (2008). Indian companies with solutions that the world needs: sustainability as a driver for innovation and profit. New Delhi: CII-ITC CESD.

6
Indonesia

Jimmy Tanaya
Research Director, Centre for Innovation Policy and Governance, Indonesia

Juniati Gunawan
Director, Trisakti Sustainability Center, Trisakti University, Indonesia

Semerdanta Pusaka
Director, PT Aicón Global Indonesia, Indonesia

Yanuar Nugroho
Research Fellow, Manchester Business School, UK

National context

Indonesia is an archipelagic nation of 17,508 islands (6,000 inhabited) covering 1.9 million km² (65% of which is water). Based on the 2010 census, Indonesia had about 237,6 million people and 1,128 ethnicities; the majority religion was Islam (87.1%), followed by Protestantism (6.9%), Catholicism (2.9%), Hinduism (1.7%), Buddhism (0.7%), and other beliefs (0.7%). It is estimated that the population will grow to about 255 million in 2015. Indonesian GDP and GDP growth in 2013 were Rp 2,770.3 trillion (c. US$231 billion) and 5.78% with manufacturing, agriculture, stock husbandry, forestry, and fisheries industry sectors as the largest contributors to the economy (BPS, 2014).

Situated on the Pacific Ocean's "ring of fire", Indonesia is prone to natural hazards such as tsunamis, flash floods, earthquakes and volcanic eruptions. Indonesia also faces anthropogenic risks, such as forest burning, deforestation, pollution and business human rights malpractices. This is partly as a result of regulatory frameworks in Indonesia, which have long been in favour of low wages and weak environmental regulations. Therefore, promoting sustainable enterprise initiatives is a daunting challenge for the government, business and civil society.

Priority issues

Indonesia faces various social challenges, including conflict and unrest related to land tenure, and issues relating to crime, violence, bullying, health and wellbeing, consumptive lifestyles and low work ethic (Pawennei *et al.*, 2013, p. 229). Indonesia scores 0.684 and is ranked 108 out of 187 countries on the UN Human Development Index, while 20.8% of the population lives in multi-dimensional poverty (Malik, 2014). Income inequality is high, as indicated by a Gini Index score of 38.1 (World Bank, 2013) and unemployment is 6.6% (BPS, 2013).

Political issues include inadequate regulations, lack of good governance, election fraud, weak law enforcement, high levels of bureaucracy, a declining R&D budget and uncertain political stability (Buckley and Mwamadzingo, 2012; Pawennei *et al.*, 2013, p. 228). Indonesia's score and rank on Transparency's Corruption Perceptions Index is 34 and 107 in 2014 (Transparency International, 2014).

There are various sustainability challenges associated with the growth of extractives, palm oil and property sectors. Many environmental impacts are linked to illegal and excessive exploitation of natural resources, land conversion, water extraction and the impact of climate change on the agri-business and fishery industries. Public transport in the big cities is poor and there is an energy crisis, with demand outstripping supply and renewable energy sources yet to be deployed.

Trends

The mainstreaming of sustainability issues indicates a gradual shift towards sustainable enterprise, influenced by the material concerns of stakeholders, such as workers and consumers. For most companies, however, this manifests as philanthropy or CSR, reflecting a risk mitigation and prevention perspective (Tanaya, 2013). One area where there has been the most dramatic progress is sustainability reporting.

In 2008, around 27% of 376 listed companies in the Jakarta Stock Exchange engaged in CSR reporting (Nugroho *et al.*, 2010), compared with 94% of 484 listed companies in 2013. The major shift towards sustainability reporting is driven by two factors: compliance to related regulations and the pursuit for corporate reputation. For example, nonfinancial disclosure is endorsed by Government Regulation Number 47 of 2012 and the Chairman of Capital Market and Financial Institution Supervisory Agency's Decree Number KEP-134/BL/2006.

Government policies

Indonesia was one of the first countries to make Corporate Social Responsibility (CSR) mandatory (Nugroho *et al.*, 2010). This applies mainly to companies with significant impacts on natural resources (Law Number 40 of 2007, especially Article 74), and foreign investors (Law Number 25 of 2007, particularly Article 15 (b), Article 16 and 34). This law requires all foreign investors to take into account good governance, fair operating practices, environment protection, employees' welfare, occupational health and safety, and compliance to regulations.

Article 74 of Law Number 40 of 2007 defines Social and Environment Responsibility as a corporate commitment to contribute actively to sustainable economic development in order to develop quality of life and the environment in ways that bring benefits to the company, local community, and society at large. However, the laws do not go further to delineate requirements such as company size, budget, and CSR initiatives.

Other relevant legislation includes stipulations for state-owned enterprises (in terms of PER-08/MBU/2013 of 2013) on nine sustainability topics, namely: disaster relief and recovery, education, health, public infrastructure, religious facility, environmental conservation, transportation for workers, poverty alleviation, and partnership/financial aid. The Regulation of Indonesia Investment Coordinating Board (BKPM) Number 3 of 2012 also asserts that investors should carry out and report on CSR.

There is an ongoing process led by the National Standardization Agency of Indonesia (BSN) to turn ISO 26000 into an Indonesian National Standard (SNI). Moreover, there are a number of international and national certification regimes based on commodities that shape sustainable business practices in Indonesia, e.g. Roundtable on Sustainable Palm Oil's Certified Sustainable Palm Oil (CSPO). There were around 5.5 million tonnes CSPO (16.67%) of 33 million tonnes total palm oil produced in Indonesia in 2014.

Case studies

Antam (PT Aneka Tambang (Persero))

Antam was established in 1968 through a merger of several mining companies. It is a publicly listed company with 65% ownership held by the Indonesian Government and 35% owned by the public. As a mining company, one of the biggest sustainability challenges is to minimize the negative impacts of a mine closure, which is done through a phased, planned process. Antam's post-mining programmes include reclamation and revegetation, acceleration of local economic growth, capacity building for farmers, promotion of integrated animal husbandry and fishery, and development of local business associations and microfinance cooperatives. Antam's integrated agricultural programme, called "Low External Input Sustainable Agriculture", maximizes the use of waste as raw materials. The company is piloting an integrated farming system on sandy land, in cooperation with local business groups and cooperatives.

Arus Liar (PT Lintas Jeram Nusantara)

Arus Liar is an adventure tourism operator, specialized in rafting and outdoor management training packages. Formal alignment of Arus Liar's business strategy with sustainability began in 2010 when it joined an action research project on ISO 26000. In terms of creating shared value, Arus Liar hires almost 100% of employees from local areas, buys products from local suppliers and empowers local sandal producers. Several small shops and restaurants have also been established to serve its customers. The company supports environmental conservation of the Citarik River through education and tree planting activities. Arus Liar has also been involved in a number of Search and Rescue missions as a part of its corporate volunteering programme. In recognition of these activities, Arus Liar won the Leading Responsible Tourism in the Indonesia Travel and Tourism Awards (ITTA) 2012/13.

Express Group

Express Group is the second largest taxi operator in Indonesia, founded in 1989, which operates a partnership scheme with 3,500 drivers. Under the scheme, drivers make a small down payment for a taxi, which converted into a full ownership after a certain service period. The use of a Global Positioning System (GPS) and Digital Dispatch System (DDS) cuts fuel consumption by 15%. There are about 22 taxi pools where Express provides an opportunity to 264 SMEs to provide services to taxi drivers. In addition, Express supports the Indonesian Care for Children with Cancer Foundation (YKAKI) by providing shuttle services for children going for cancer therapy to and from five hospitals in Jakarta's area and Bali. To address environmental challenges and global warming, Express also has planted 10,000 trees in cooperation with other organizations.

SMART (Sinar Mas Agro Resources and Technology)

SMART is a subsidiary of Golden Agri-Resources Ltd (GAR) – one of the largest palm-based companies in the world. Established in 1962, SMART currently holds around 138,800 ha of oil palm plantations including smallholders. SMART is also tasked to manage all of GAR's 472,800 ha of palm oil plantations as of 31 December 2014. In 2009, Greenpeace launched a campaign to boycott SMART on the basis of deforestation and endangering orang-utan. The campaign was followed by purchase suspensions from a number of buyers including Unilever, Nestlé, Abengoa Bioenergy and Burger King during the period of 2009–10.

In order to answer the allegation, SMART and GAR appointed independent auditors to examine the allegation in 2010 and pioneered the Forest Conservation Policy (FCP) in 2011. The FCP, developed by GAR in collaboration with The Forest Trust and Greenpeace, maintains that GAR would no longer develop palm oil plantations on high carbon stock forests, high conservation value forest areas and peat-lands. It addition, it would show respect for indigenous and local communities and compliance with all relevant laws and the National Interpretation of RSPO's Principles and Criteria.

As such, SMART's plantations have gradually obtained CSPO certification since 2013. Furthermore, Greenpeace's report in 2014 suggests that GAR has made a number of improvements over the years. Other big companies such as Wilmar, Cargill, Asian Agri, and Asia Pulp and Paper (GAR's sister company) have also followed GAR's lead and built on their own FCP (Greenpeace, 2014).

Further resources

Indonesia Business Council for Sustainable Development (IBCSD) – An association led by CEOs in Indonesia and affiliated to the World Business Council for Sustainable Development (WBCSD) to promote sustainable economic growth, ecological balance and social progress.

Indonesia Global Compact Network (IGCN) – A network of institutions affiliated with the United Nations Global Compact (UNGC).

Indonesia Chamber of Commerce and Industry – The umbrella organization of Indonesian business chambers and associations, which has a specific department that manages social and CSR issues.

International Society of Sustainability Professionals – The Indonesia Chapter is an affiliation of ISSP International based in the USA and is a professional association working on sustainability issues.

References

BPS (2013). National labour force survey 2004, 2005, 2006, 2007, 2008, 2009, 2010, 2011, 2012, and 2013. Jakarta, Indonesia: Biro Pusat Statistik.

BPS (2014). Berita resmi statistik No.16/02/Th.XVII, 5 February 2014. Jakarta, Indonesia: Biro Pusat Statistik.

Buckley, G. & Mwamadzingo, M. (2012). Indonesia: an enabling environment for sustainable enterprises (EESE) assessment and a survey on workers' perceptions *Employment Sector, Employment Report No. 16*. Geneva: ILO, International Labour Office, Employment Sector, Small Enterprise Programme, Job Creation and Enterprise Development Department.

Greenpeace (2014). Golden agri resources: a progress report. Amsterdam, the Netherlands: Greenpeace International.

Malik, K. (2014). Human development report 2014. Sustaining human progress: reducing vulnerabilities and building resilience. New York: United Nations Development Programme.

Nugroho, Y., Tanaya, J., Widiyanti, T. & Permana, A.H. (2010). Indonesia. In W. Visser & N. Tolhurst (Eds.), *World Guide to CSR: A Country-by-Country Analysis of Corporate Sustainability and Responsibility* (pp. 198-203). Sheffield, UK: Greenleaf Publishing.

Pawennei, I.A., Sari, V.A., Usmani, M.L. & Esti, K. (2013). Horizon scanning: pemetaan events dan trends daerah (EN: Horizon scanning: mapping of regional events and trends). Jakarta, Indonesia: CIPG.

Tanaya, J. (2013). Corporate social responsibility: a framework for analysing CSR heterogeneity through the case of Indonesian palm oil. Faculty of Humanities, Manchester Business School. Manchester, The University of Manchester, Manchester, UK.

Transparency International (2014). Corruption perceptions index 2014. Berlin, Germany: Transparency International.

World Bank (2013). World development indicators. Washington, DC: The World Bank.

7
Japan

Kazunori Kobayashi
CEO, EcoNetworks Co., Japan

National context

Japanese society, widely admired for its cohesiveness and harmony, is moving through rough terrain and needs innovation now more than ever to overcome looming social issues.

The country's well-earned prosperity is also not without a downside as the current culture of consumerism is clearly unsustainable. It would require 2.3 Earths for the world to enjoy the same living standards as the average Japanese (WWF, 2010). Meanwhile, the mix of a declining birth rate, rising average age, and a growing population of older people have placed Japan at the forefront of "greying societies" around the world.

After the devastating 2011 Tohoku earthquake, major issues remain with the nuclear clean-up and restoration of the liveability of the stricken region, as well as growing social movements to reformulate the nation's energy infrastructure.

The good news is that some very clever entrepreneurs are applying the spirit of innovation to sustainable enterprise. Thousands of local entrepreneurs are moving to address these issues and actively build social businesses, most of which are local, responsive and designed for the circular economy, but limited in size.

Established corporations are also being called on and are gradually responding to move corporate social responsibility (CSR) into the DNA of their core businesses in the form of "value creation CSR" or "creating shared value" (CSV). These more traditional entities are better positioned to provide scalability but have been weak in terms of circularity and responsiveness.

The challenge ahead is for sustainable enterprises to emerge and develop beyond social businesses and CSR/CSV and take root in the mainstream.

Priority issues

One quarter of the Japanese population is currently 65 years or older and this percentage is expected to grow to 40% by 2055 (CAO, 2007). It seems inevitable, with a ratio of one older person to 1.2 people under 65, that Japanese people will come under increasing pressure to work in their 70s and 80s. The social security system's sustainability is under threat as pensions, medical care, nursing care and other welfare service costs are expected to grow, putting further strain on a mounting national deficit.

In Japan, 2012 is often referred to as "the starting year for renewable energy". Supported by a renewable energy feed-in tariff system introduced in July that year, in just 15 months solar power generation expanded to some 5.85 GW of output – equal to six nuclear power plants (Institute for Sustainable Energy Policies, 2014). Social movements are gaining momentum for a switch to renewable energy from an energy infrastructure long reliant on nuclear energy and fossil fuels. However, it remains to be seen whether sustainable renewable energy will become a foundation for the country's energy infrastructure.

Gender equality is another priority issue. Japan ranked 104 out of 142 countries in the Global Gender Gap Report 2014. The country ranked highly for gender parity in education and health but lags in economic and political participation (World Economic Forum, 2014). The gradual progress that is being made is impeded by long work hours and entrenched work customs, which are legacies of the male-centric economic success paradigm. Diversity and inclusion remain major challenges.

Trends

A Ministry of Economy, Trade, and Industry survey (2008) estimated that social business is a ¥240 billion (US$2.4 billion) industry encompassing 8,000 companies in Japan. The number of social businesses has certainly increased substantially since then, but no recent statistics have been published. The government plans to release its first nationwide social business industry survey in 2015.

Typical focus areas for social enterprises were revealed by a survey of 100 small and medium enterprises, non-profit organizations (NPOs) and other entities, namely: independent living of people with disabilities, promotion of agriculture and nature, environmental protection and remediation, international cooperation, local revitalization, medical and health, support for low-income earners, social business support, independent living of the elderly and childcare support. The report also identified common hurdles faced by these enterprises, including a lack of tax and government support, inability to provide competitive salaries and insufficient networks for funding and organizational know-how (GISPRI and E-Square Inc., 2011).

A survey by Entrepreneurial Training for Innovative Communities (2013) found that 64% of people aged 20–39 were familiar with the terms "social business" and "social entrepreneur", suggesting that the concept holds a significant level of attention among younger generations who are inevitably more sensitive to sustainability and other social issues.

A 2012 report by the Japan Association of Corporate Executives stated that the rehabilitation and reconstruction efforts after the Tohoku earthquake made most corporations become aware that the management of their core operations must provide for both ongoing social contribution and business growth.

Government policies

Japan currently has no legal institutional or tax framework designed to accommodate the specific needs of sustainable enterprises or social businesses. Hence, they adopt a variety of forms, from NPOs and limited companies to proprietorships and associations (Laratta *et al.*, 2011). NPOs are the most common but most NPOs receive no preferential tax treatment other than being taxed only on profitable activities.

The Ministry of Economy, Trade and Industry became aware of the potential of social business to create new regional industries and employment in 2008. Since then, it has provided support by recognizing and rewarding progressive achievements, holding nationwide forums, and through its Social Business Network serving as a hub for communication and promotion.

Reforms to the regulation of Japan's electricity generation came into effect in 2013 with an amendment to the Electricity Business Act, which allows full retail supply competition starting in 2016 and the splitting of the transmission and distribution sectors in 2018 (METI, 2014). At the local government level, Tokyo plans to use 25% renewable energy by 2020, and Fukushima Prefecture is aiming for 100% by 2040. In addition, the Ministry of the Environment began providing support for locally led renewable energy businesses in 2011.

Positive action is also being implemented to redress gender disparities in the country, and the government has set a target for women to hold over 30% of leadership positions in all social sectors by 2020.

Case studies

Aizu Electric Power Company

In the aftermath of the 2011 earthquake and nuclear disaster in the Fukushima region, Yaemon Sato gathered a coalition of local business people in 2013 to create Aizu Electric Power. The company's business model is to use local renewable resources to produce and supply energy and help re-establish the local economy and culture.

In March 2014, the company opened a citizen contribution fund to enable social participation in financing a plan to build 21 small-scale on-site solar power generation facilities producing 1.45MW of electricity. In the future, the company plans to build small hydroelectric and biomass power stations fuelled by timber from forest thinning and to sell surplus energy to the municipal power companies. The local citizens and business community are strongly embracing the plan for its grand vision of applying the region's abundant resources to meeting the prefectural government's 2012 pledge to switch to 100% renewable energy by 2040.

Sato has experience splicing into infrastructure controlled by entrenched oligopolies. A ninth-generation sake brewer in a lineage begun in 1790, he is the chairman of the Japan Jizake Cooperative and successfully rallied independent makers of local sake (*jizaké*) during a recent boom in popularity to get their one-of-a-kind spirits into the sales routes dominated by the mega-brewers.

The fragility and safety of Japan's power generation infrastructure became an acute national issue after the nuclear disaster, and community movements have led to over 50 new community power operators since the disaster. In 2014, these operators created the Local Power Generators Network, which launched the Fukushima Community Power Declaration at a meeting of the Institute for Sustainable Energy Policies, calling for collective action to accelerate social innovation through community power.

Irodori

The mountain town of Kamikatsu was struggling with an ageing society and depopulation. When import liberalization and severe weather virtually wiped out the town's core forestry and clementine industries, Tomoji Yokoichi, a member of the local agricultural cooperative, devised a business model to meet the needs of both the market and local workforce.

In 1986, with the town itself as the principal shareholder, Yokoichi launched Irodori to supply leaves harvested primarily by senior citizens to premier Japanese restaurants nationwide for use as garnish with their meals. In 2012, Irodori reported ¥230 million (US$2.3 million) in sales and represented 80% of the national leaf garnish market.

The "leaf business" combines a highly renewable natural resource with an enthusiastic staff of 200 farmers of an average age over 70, with the eldest 94. An information system specially designed for use by its older-aged staff provides direct access to market information giving them control over product quality, order fulfilment and delivery. The highly experienced employees – often a marginalized sector of society – are grateful to have meaningful work that lets them be actively employed and financially independent. Some even earn more than ¥10 million (US$100,000) annually.

The renewed vitality that the staff and town is gaining as the business grows is resulting in fewer applications for assisted living residences to the point that municipally operated residences are no longer needed. Annually some 4,000 visitors from Japan and abroad come to observe this innovative social business in a greying society.

ISFnet Group

Yukiyoshi Watanabe founded ISFnet in 2000 to provide IT support services using trained cohorts of professional IT engineers from economically marginalized sectors of society, such as NEETs (Not in Education, Employment or Training), underemployed workers, single parents and primary caregivers, socially withdrawn people and senior citizens.

ISFnet has since expanded its recruitment policy to its "Target 20" social groups, including refugees and victims of domestic violence, who for various reasons experience barriers to employment. The company estimates that about 40% of its staff belong to one of these groups.

In 2014, ISFnet had grown to an organization with over 1,600 employees and annual sales of ¥7.7 billion (US$77 million). ISFnet also has a company in the group called ISFnet Harmony (started in 2008), which provides a work environment designed specifically for people with physical, intellectual and mental disabilities. The business model transferred well, as ISFnet Harmony achieved profitability in just two years and the company plans to continue growing to provide long-term employment to over 1,000 people with disabilities by 2020.

ISFnet's ingenuity in creating infrastructure and work environments that harness each individual's skills and strengths is opening eyes in the way employment is viewed in Japan.

Further resources

Entrepreneurial Training for Innovative Communities – One of the leading leadership development programme and networking institution for young social entrepreneurs. More than new 150 entrepreneurs are "born" out of their training programmes.

Japan Association of Corporate Executives – Formed in 1946 and promotes corporate social responsibility under the banner "corporations are public institutions serving society".

Network of Business Leaders and Entrepreneurs for a Sustainable Business and Energy Future – Established in 2013 as a connecting point for collaboration on issues related to sustainable energy and business by the public, government and corporate sectors with about 300 organizations and individuals.

Shinrai Zaidan – A public interest charitable organization providing interest-free, unsecured financing to social businesses and conducting forums and networking events designed to build trust in the social business community.

Social Business Network – Formed in 2010 as Japan's first business association promoting social business for a sustainable society, gathers 200 progressive social businesses and entrepreneurs.

Social Innovator Koshien – An influential forum supported by a long list of government agencies and social innovation companies.

References

CAO (2007). White paper on the aging society (summary) FY 2007. Tokyo: Government of Japan.

Entrepreneurial Training for Innovative Communities (2013). Recognition among youth in social business and entrepreneur survey. Report. Tokyo: Entrepreneurial Training for Innovative Communities.

GISPRI (Global Industrial and Social Progress) & E-Square Inc. (2011). Survey on social businesses by SMEs and NPOs. Report, Tokyo.

Institute for Sustainable Energy Policies (2014). Renewables Japan status report 2014 executive summary. Report. Tokyo: Institute for Sustainable Energy Policies.

Laratta, R., Nakagawa, S. & Sakurai, M. (2011). Japanese social enterprises: major contemporary issues and key challenges. *Social Enterprise Journal*, 7(1), 50-68.

Ministry of Economy, Trade, and Industry (METI) (2008). Social business working group report: the state of social business. Report, Tokyo: Government of Japan.

Ministry of Economy, Trade, and Industry (METI) (2014). *Electricity system reform*. Report, Tokyo: Government of Japan.

World Economic Forum (2014). *The global gender gap report 2014*. Report, Cologny: WEF.

WWF (2010). Japan's ecological footprint. Tokyo: WWF.

Acknowledgements

Editorial assistance by Stephen Ballati.

8
Kazakhstan

Azhar Baisakalova
Assistant Professor in Public Policy and Management, Department of Public
Administration, KIMEP University, Kazakhstan

National context

Kazakhstan is a former communist country and emerging economy, where
the CSR agenda is influenced by its historical, cultural, political and development factors. Kazakhstan, with 17 million people on its vast territory
of 2.7 million km², has a diversity of abundant minerals, including zinc,
tungsten, barite, silver, lead, chrome ironstone, copper, molybdenum,
uranium and gold. In addition, its oil and gas reserves are among the top
ten in the world. Kazakhstan participates in major international initiatives
and institutions. It is a member of the Customs Union and the Eurasian
Economic Union with Russia and Belarus. In 2013 Kazakhstan joined the
Extractive Industries Transparency Initiative, and soon it will also be part of
the World Trade Organization.

Kazakhstan has set an ambitious goal to be among the 30 top world
economies by 2050 (Nazarbayev, 2012). As one of the major players in the
post-Soviet region, Kazakhstan has had stable economic growth over the
last 15 years. GDP growth before the world financial crisis was more than
7% and has been around 5% a year since 2009. The country's ranking in
the WEF Overall Global Competitiveness Index rose from 72 in 2011 to
50 in 2013, while its Ease of Doing Business ranking improved from 58 in
2011 to 49 in 2013. In 2013, credit rating agencies Standard & Poor's, Fitch

Group, and Moody's rated Kazakhstan as stable and positive. Consequently, Kazakhstan is a leader in attracting Foreign Direct Investment among the Commonwealth of Independent Countries. The nomination of Astana – the capital of Kazakhstan – as host city for EXPO 2017 has also increased the country's commitment to Green Economy development ideas.

Priority issues

Intensive extractive activities and the construction of pipelines, roads, railways and refineries have created significant environmental impacts, such as waste stockpiles, greenhouse gas emissions and pollution of air, water and soil. According to national statistical data sources, in 2013 the amount of accumulated solid municipal waste was about 100 million tonnes, and air polluting emissions from stationary sources constituted 2,282,700 tonnes.

In some regions access to fresh water is problematic. Industrial activities such as mining, construction, transportation, irrigation and deforestation have also contributed to desertification and land degradation. Kazakhstan's strategy for moving towards a "green economy" is focused on energy efficiency and alternative energy development, improving air quality, more efficient use of water and effective management of all types of waste. Although in 2013 the percentage of renewable energy production was only 0.3%, by the year of 2030 it is planned to increase to 30%.

In 2013 the UNDP Human Development Report ranked Kazakhstan as 69th out of 187 countries. The 2013–14 Global Competitiveness Report by the World Economic Forum (GCR WEF) identifies an inadequately educated workforce as one of the challenges for doing business in Kazakhstan, ranking the country 87th out of 148 on innovation and sophistication. The Global Innovation Index Report (Cornell University, INSEAD and WIPO, 2013) ranked Kazakhstan 84th out of 142 countries. The local content requirements create challenges for employers as finding qualified staff, good quality local products and suppliers is difficult, especially for technical personnel and in rural areas (OECD, 2014). Another serious challenge for doing business in Kazakhstan is corruption: in 2013, its Corruption Perceptions Index ranking was 140th out of 177 countries (where a rank of first is least corrupt).

Trends

Interest in CSR in Kazakhstan is increasing. For example, there is a project aimed at the development of a National Concept for promoting CSR in Kazakhstan (supported by the Netherlands) and another for developing a CSR course for higher educational institutions (supported by Norway). However, in Kazakhstan business responsibility is predominantly in the philanthropy stage, with some features of marketing and management approaches (Visser, 2012). Typically, companies support projects supplying services, such as the funding and building of schools, kindergartens, hospitals, sports facilities, and the provision of clean water in communities.

A recent study (Baisakalova, 2014) shows convergence and divergence in CSR understanding by key CSR actors in Kazakhstan. Business and trade unions' prime concern is internal responsibility, i.e. responsibility towards employees, while the state ranks internal responsibility alongside with environmental responsibilities as the second most important. Business also ranks environmental responsibilities as the second most important. The state prioritizes external responsibility, while NGOs prioritize stakeholder responsibilities. Business and NGOs rank philanthropic responsibilities towards society and community or external responsibility third, while economic responsibilities are ranked fourth.

Government policies

Kazakhstan 2050 sets a national strategic goal for the country to become one of the 30 top world economies. It envisages development based on innovative economic and social principles taking into account modern global, regional and local challenges. The priority for national policy is stable economic growth, fighting corruption, the creation of favourable conditions for sustainable business and fostering innovation (Nazarbayev, 2012).

The triple focus of economy–energy–environment is reflected in various initiatives, including the Road Map of Scientific and Technological Development for the Oil and Gas Industry to 2025, the Green Economy Concept, the Programme on Combating Desertification in the Republic of Kazakhstan 2005–15, the Astana Water Action for 2012–15, the State Programme of Water Management for 2014–40 and Astana Green Bridge Initiative.

Local content regulations require that 1% of any project budget be set aside for training programmes and workforce development. Beginning from 2014, 1% of GDP will be spent on the development of green technologies to create new, environmentally friendly and economically efficient industries. Structural changes in the economy are aimed at increasing non-oil exports from 32% to 70% of GDP. Public officials have also begun to refer to such concepts as extended producer responsibility, closed-loop (circular) economy and multicycle use of products.

Case studies

JSC KEGOC

JSC "KEGOC" is a company managing the National Power Grid of Kazakhstan and operating the Unified Power System of Kazakhstan. Its environmental policy is aimed at minimizing negative impacts on the environment, ensuring environmental protection as well as energy saving and rational use of natural resources. KEGOC provides disclosure of comprehensive information about its operations, ownership and management structure. In 2013 JSC KEGOC took the lead in the development of Kazakhstan's first business guidebook on CSR and sustainable development, entitled *CSR for Electric and Energy Companies to Increase Business Effectiveness*. The book, published in 2014, clarifies the basic concepts and trends in CSR development and highlights CSR best practices in the world and in Kazakhstan. It is a good asset for practitioners, academics and students.

JSC SEVKAZENERGO

SEVKAZENERGO is a vertically integrated company providing energy generation, transmission and supply in northern Kazakhstan. The company has published sustainable development reports since 2010. Innovations and reconstruction of technical facilities has significantly reduced pollution of air and soil from NO_x, SO_x, dust and ashes, as well as surface and groundwater quality. Installation of modern titanic emulsifiers resulted in reduction of dust emissions from 20,736 tonnes in 2008 to 3,455 tonnes in 2013. Water recycling is used for reduction of its consumption. The company is a winner of the national Paryz award in the category of "Contribution to Environment Protection".

MCO "KazMicroFinance" LLC

MCO "KazMicroFinance" LLC has 14 branches all over Kazakhstan, which provide services to more than 100,000 customers. To make microcredit easy and accessible for a greater number of people, KMF offers non-collateral loans for solidarity groups of people, who cannot get loans from other financial institutions. This facility helps 71% of clients to access finance. The company's mission, supported by its employees, is to improve the welfare of the population, especially the 61% of clients in rural areas and the 70% of clients who are women.

Smart Astana Project

This project has been launched as part of the preparation for hosting the EXPO-2017 in Astana city, the capital of Kazakhstan. The main purpose of the project is to improve the living standards and welfare of the residents of the city, to modernize its infrastructure and to improve public safety and security. All energy will be provided by renewable sources and power will be stored using innovative technologies. Renewable energy technologies, including wind, solar and earth, will be incorporated into the development, a global model for the design and operation of next-generation smart grids, distributed generation technologies, and energy storage in future cities. The project is based on following the best models of European smart cities, including promoting a smart economy, administration, life, mobility, people and environment. The smart city pilot system of improved monitoring has already improved safety and security, while smart land and smart water projects are expected to reduce consumption of energy by 20% and water by 13%.

Tengizchevroil (TCO)

In order to understand community needs in the areas of its business operations, TCO initiated a social baseline assessment in 2008. The survey revealed a number of serious social issues in education, health, youth culture and recreation, as well as the lack of active NGOs. In 2009, TCO partnered with a corporate fund, the Eurasia Foundation Central Asia (EFCA), to launch its Community Engagement Programme. The initial stages of the project successfully pursued a multitude of goals, from raising test scores in area schools to training doctors to work more collaboratively with patients. As a result, 58 key community leaders have been trained, ten

NGOs created, 48 training sessions provided to the wider community and 11 youth leadership clubs created at schools. The programme supports the sustained growth of initiatives by both individuals and NGOs.

Further resources

Eurasia Foundation in Central Asia (Almaty) – A corporate fund, which initiated the development of the National Concept for Promoting Corporate Social Responsibility in Kazakhstan. The concept provides recommendations for the implementation of corporate social responsibility principles and standards not only for the business community and government, but also for all groups of civil society.

KazEnergy Association – Established to create favourable conditions for the dynamic and sustainable development of the energy sector of the Republic of Kazakhstan. It serves as an integrated information hub for subsoil users, energy and transport specialists and consumers of products and services of oil and gas and electric power industry.

National Chamber of Entrepreneurs – Strongly supports the National Concept for Promoting CSR and was active in its finalization. In June 2014 a draft was presented at the Global Forum for Responsible Business Conduct organized by the OECD and held in Paris, France. The draft Concept has been submitted to the Government of the Republic of Kazakhstan.

References

Baisakalova, A.B. (2014). Comparative study of perceptions of corporate social responsibility by different stakeholders in emerging markets. *Journal of Global Management* 7(1), 1-19.

Cornell University, INSEAD & WIPO (2013). The Global Innovation Index 2013: The Local Dynamics of Innovation. Geneva, Ithaca and Fontainebleau.

Nazarbayev, N.A. (2012). Address by the President of the Republic of Kazakhstan, Leader of the Nation. *Strategy Kazakhstan-2050*.

OECD (2014). *Responsible Business Conduct in Kazakhstan*, OECD Publishing.

UNDP (2013). *Human Development Report*. New York: United Nations Development Programme.

Visser, W. (2012). The future of CSR: towards transformative CSR, or CSR 2.0. *Kaleidoscope Futures Paper Series*, 1.

WEF (2014). *The Global Competitiveness Report 2013–2014*. Geneva: World Economic Forum.

9
Malaysia

Theresa Bauer
Professor of International Management and Marketing, SRH FernHochschule Riedlingen, Germany

Azlan Amran
Associate Professor, Universiti Sains Malaysia, Malaysia

National context

Since independence in 1957, Malaysia has been a federal constitutional elective monarchy. The country covers two main regions: Peninsular Malaysia and Malaysian Borneo. Its population of 28 million represents a multiracial society with a Malay majority, large Chinese and Indian minorities and a number of aboriginal groups.

The country is rich in natural resources such as oil, tin and palm oil, which form the basis for socioeconomic development. More recently, the economy has expanded into other sectors such as tourism. Malaysia's economic growth is relatively competitive compared to other Asian countries. The gross national income per capita was US$8,194, or about US$16,201 in purchasing power parity (PPP), in 2010. In per capita terms, the economy achieved average growth of 8.0% a year from 1970 to 2010.

The government supports the idea of sustainable development and has started efforts to raise awareness about sustainable production and consumption. In 2009, at the COP15 in Copenhagen, Malaysia made a conditional commitment to reduce carbon emission intensity of Malaysian GDP by up to 40% by 2020 from a 2005 baseline. Malaysia has been recognized as an early pioneer in environmental policy; however, several areas remain in need of improvement. The number of companies that integrate sustainability and responsibility into strategy, operations and products is still limited, but rising.

Priority issues

Malaysia is a developing country heading towards industrialization. Its economic development has benefited many Malaysians. For instance, household poverty has steadily decreased in rural and urban areas and total household poverty incidence is lower than 5%.

Malaysia's rapid economic growth is having a significant impact on the environment, especially rising carbon dioxide emissions. Malaysia has been experiencing a warming trend in the past few decades, and the annual mean temperature is projected to increase by 1.5–2.0°C by 2050 (NRE, 2011). With the temperature rise, it has been projected that malarial and dengue vector mosquitoes will follow, resulting in greater transmission of these diseases (NRE, 2011).

It has been projected that Malaysia's total demand for energy will grow at an annual rate of 4.8% from 2000 to 2020 (NRE, 2011). As an initiative towards sustainable development, Malaysia encourages renewable energy resources such as solar, wind, hydro and biomass. However, Malaysia achieved only 20% of its renewable energy target in its Ninth Malaysia Plan (originally set at 350 MW of electricity generated from renewable energy) by 2010 (Hashim and Ho, 2011).

With rapid urbanization, building sustainable cities is currently one of the major challenges. For example, water resources must be managed efficiently and water conservation efforts such as rainwater harvesting are needed.

Trends

Awareness and commitment to sustainability practices have been growing since the mandatory requirement to report Corporate Social Responsibility activities was instituted following the Prime Minister's budget speech in

2006 and the introduction of the CSR framework by the Malaysian stock exchange, Bursa Malaysia, in 2007.

A survey conducted by CSR Asia shows that CSR is increasing in prevalence among leading companies in the Asia–Pacific region, whereas the CSR reporting of Malaysian companies ranks sixth among the top ten Asian countries (BERNAMA, 2009). The companies were rated against 51 indicators, and Malaysia scored 60% for governance, codes and policies; 23% for CSR strategy and communication; 34% for marketplace and supply chain; 27% for workplace and people; 28% for environment; and 39% for community and development. According to the Global Reporting Initiative, the number of Malaysian companies which report their sustainability practices increased from four in 2008 to 17 in 2013.

Green technologies are being developed, and some manufacturing companies have begun to embrace sustainable supply chain management practices such as environmental purchasing and packaging, mostly in an effort to gain competitive advantages, or as a response to government incentives or pressure from foreign parent companies.

Areas for improvement remain. Many company leaders do not consider environmental issues a part of their firm's strategy, as, for example, a recent survey among logisticians revealed (Zailani *et al.*, 2011). One of the dominant sectors of the Malaysian economy, the palm oil industry, has a bad reputation regarding its environmental impact and must deal with its specific challenges. So far, circa 20% of the local palm oil industry is under the Roundtable on Sustainable Palm Oil (RSPO) certification (see Adnan, 2014); in addition, the Malaysian Sustainable Palm Oil (MSPO) standard was launched in 2014 to meet the necessities of mid-sized and small producers.

Government policies

The Malaysian government is committed to moving forward towards a sustainable economy. It has embarked on a number of national transformation programmes such as the Government Transformation Programme (GTP), the Economic Transformation Programme (ETP), the New Economic Model (NEM) and the Tenth Malaysia Plan (10MP). These national policies serve to position Malaysia to become a high-income, developed nation that is inclusive and sustainable by 2020. For example, the NEM that was unveiled in 2010 aims at stimulating economic growth by improving worker productivity across all sectors, with an eye towards sustainability.

Several other policies have been enacted and formulated to strengthen the institutional framework, including, for example the National Environmental Policy, National Climate Change Policy, National Green Technology Policy, National Policy on Biological Diversity, Renewable Energy Policy and Action Plan, and Environmental Quality Act.

In 2010, the government announced a US$30 million CSR fund and a US$0.46 billion Green Technology Fund for the promotion of research and development towards environmental sustainability. A federal-level Ministry of Energy, Green Technology and Water has been created. In November 2013, Prime Minister Najib Razak announced a US$6 million social business fund, promising support for the fledgling social enterprise sector.

Although Malaysia has been recognized as an early pioneer in environmental policy, the findings by Kairul Nadim *et al.* (2013) show that inconsistencies and challenges remain, such as the need to better coordinate among stakeholders, the need to harmonize policy objectives and the need to synergize the various instruments, initiatives and programmes.

Case studies

Biji-biji Initiative

Small recycling enterprises are nothing new in Malaysia. After independence in 1957, a number of individuals made their living by buying and reselling used bottles, cooking utensils and old batteries. While this business used to be low-profit and little accepted, recycling is now welcomed as a way to reduce usage of raw materials that can take on creative forms. Biji-biji Initiative is a social enterprise founded by four young Malaysians who manufacture products such as door gifts for company events and festival booths from discarded material. The initiative started in January 2013 by using social media to obtain unwanted materials, such as old wood and advertising banners. The collaborative group is committed to an open-source approach and encourages the public's participation in the production process. It has been awarded the Arthur Guinness Fund and British Council Social Enterprise Award.

Global Green Synergy (GGS)

In light of repeated criticism of the palm oil industry, some companies have started efforts to make the industry more sustainable, for example, by transforming carbon sources into carbon sinks. Global Green Synergy (GGS) treats and processes oil palm biomass to produce value-added products. Dried Long Fiber is produced from the empty fruit bunch that is considered a waste product after the fresh fruit bunch has been processed. Dried Long Fiber is biodegradable and can be used, for example, in mattress and cushion production, paper and pulp production and acoustics control. Other products offered by GGS include briquettes and pellets, compost, and palm kernel shell charcoal. GGS also undertakes research and development projects in cooperation with private and public institutions.

Iskandar Malaysia

Iskandar is a 2.217 km^2 development corridor in Johor, Malaysia, where economic activities focus on electronics, logistics, food, agriculture and tourism. In line with the Malaysian government's aspiration to reduce carbon intensity, Iskandar has been planned as an environment-friendly, socially responsible metropolitan region. A Low Carbon Society Blueprint for Iskandar Malaysia 2025 has been developed in a joint effort of experts, policy-makers and communities. The blueprint outlines 12 actions to reduce carbon emissions, including integrated green transportation, green industry, green building and construction, a green energy system and renewable energy, sustainable waste management and a clean-air environment. The goal is to reduce the intensity of greenhouse gas emissions per unit of production by 50% by 2025 (base year 2005). Challenges remain, such as the need to raise public awareness and change people's lifestyles, as well as greater engagement by private business including the informal sector.

Wild Asia

Wild Asia is a pioneer of sustainable tourism in the region that began as a website known as Wildborneo.net in 1998 to share information on forests and communities. Today it is registered as a social enterprise that promotes sustainable tourism with the goal of combining business growth, good relationships with local communities and sustainability. The company offers advisory services and conducts training workshops with companies in the forestry, tourism and agriculture sectors, as well as sharing information and nurturing new projects to incentivize a change from within business.

Through the annual Responsible Tourism Awards, Wild Asia identifies tour operators who have adopted sustainable practices. The Awards checklist is aligned to the United Nation's World Tourism Organization's (UNWTO) Global Sustainable Tourism Criteria and acts as a showcase for exemplary resorts. Founding shareholders have signed an agreement recognizing the social mission and enterprise of Wild Asia. In line with this approach, Reza Azmi, Executive Director of Wild Asia, has established the following profit distribution formula: 65% of profits go back into the programmes and work, while 35% form a bonus incentive scheme to reward staff, advisers and associates.

Zenxin Agri-Organic Food

Demand for and supply of green products is still limited in Malaysia. Among the few organic growth vegetable suppliers is Zenxin Agri-Organic Food. Since 2001, Zenxin has produced, distributed and retailed organic products for the Malaysian and Singaporean markets. Tropical crops are grown in Malaysia and Thailand; however, seasonal temperate crops are sourced from the northern and southern hemispheres. Since 2008, the Zenxin production chain has been certified organic by the National Association for Sustainable Agriculture, Australia (NASAA). The company also offers visitors insights into the techniques and virtues of organic farming in an open-to-the-public organic farm.

Further resources

Business Council for Sustainability and Responsibility Malaysia (BCSRM) – A major advocate of Malaysia's sustainability, governance and responsibility agenda. The core activities are capacity development, awareness building, advocacy and thought leadership in these areas.

References

Adnan, H. (2014, March 8). Standard for sustainability. *The Star Online*. Retrieved from http://www.thestar.com.my/Business/Business-News/2014/03/08/Standard-for-sustainability-The-Malaysian-Sustainable-Palm-Oil-MSPO-standard-paves-the-way-for-ou/?style=biz.

BERNAMA (2009). Malaysia emerges 6th place in CSR Asia survey. 26 October 2009.

Hashim, H. & Ho, W.S. (2011). Renewable energy policies and initiatives for a sustainable energy future in Malaysia. *Renewable and Sustainable Energy Reviews*, 15: 4780-4787.

Khairul Naim, A., Merle, K. & Weihd, G. (2013). Sustainable consumption and production in Malaysia: a baseline study on government policies, institution and practices. Economic Planning Unit, Prime Minister Department, Malaysia.

NRE (2011). Malaysia second national communication to the United Nations Framework Convention on Climate Change. Ministry of Natural Resources and Environment, Malaysia.

Zailani, S., Amran, A. & Jumadi, H. (2011). Green innovation adoption among logistics service providers in Malaysia: an exploratory study on the managers' perceptions. *International Business Management*, 5, 104-113.

10
Maldives

Khadeeja Balkhi
Director of Sustainability, Balkhi Strategy Group, Pakistan

National context

Maldives' paradoxes intrigue even more than its breathtaking beauty: there were 1.2 million visitors from around the world in 2014 to a nation with a population of under 400,000 and only two cities. Maldives includes 110 resort-islands with developing costs averaging $1.5 million/room in the middle of the Indian Ocean – yet 61,000 locals scrape by on $1/day. Anything goes at the über-luxury resort-cum-playgrounds of the rich and famous – yet liquor, pork and swimsuits are banned elsewhere in this 100% Sunni Muslim country.

At $8,800, Maldives has the highest per capita GDP in the region – yet, given income disparities, most locals may not be able to stay afloat without heavy subsidies on basics ranging from food to fuel. Ninety per cent of the nation's territory is water, yet most islands suffer water-related challenges given saline groundwater and the lack of sewerage systems; 5% of the world's reefs are within this tiny archipelago, yet most Maldivians cannot swim and interact with the riches therein.

Home to a relaxed small-island culture – yet Maldives suffers the world's highest divorce rate. Behind the hype around this tiny nation, daily living tells a different story. The very seclusion that draws tourists here also creates daily hardships. Public services delivery is difficult, particularly medical and legislative. Lack of industry, economic adversity and disparity between islands, transportation and heightened environmental vulnerability are among well-documented national struggles.

Governments have adapted well to the country's only economic engine, tourism. Import duties and tourism-related taxes provide 90% of revenues, 84% from "visitor exports". At 62,500 jobs, 44% of employment is in tourism. It is now a criminal offence to call for or support a tourism boycott.

Priority issues

As a smattering of 1,200 coral islands peeking an average of 1.5 m above sea level, Maldives represents one of the planet's most endangered ecosystems, coral reefs. 200 islands are inhabited, with one-third of the population crammed on the capital, Malé. Like sea levels, tensions are rising here. Given a disproportionate focus on global warming, awareness about Maldives' real challenges is low. Balancing between income generation and protecting the environment that attracts tourists has proven tough. Fishing, mainly via the traditional, sustainable pole-and-line method, is the second largest economic activity here.

Maldives is perched on massive coral columns organically emerging as islands over millennia. Maldivian reefs are the world's seventh largest. While robust and aesthetically quaint, mining for coral chunks increases surrounding water depth, reducing tide protection against erosion. Since 1985, Maldives has also been dredging for harbour deepening, land reclamation, and construction material mining. Sand-mining is a capital intensive solution for creating new land, one that also increases susceptibility to flooding.

Thilafushi Island is the current national garbage solution. Managed by Malé, Thilafushi charges each 5-tonne garbage-carrying *dhoni* (local boat) $110. Bigger *dhonis* pay $210. Some environmentalists suggest these profits may be discouraging innovative waste management. Once a pristine lagoon, Thilafushi was reclaimed to handle growing solid waste. Reclamation couldn't keep up with the daily 330 tonnes of garbage, so waste is incinerated and dumped across the shoreline, creating new but uninhabitable land.

Thilafushi represents another Maldivian paradox: Each tourist generates up to 7.5 kg of waste a day. The 150 Bangladeshi staff work seven days a week, hand-sorting garbage without masks or gloves. With waste including putrefying food, plastic, asbestos and batteries, this is an environmental, social and public-health disaster. In the summer of 2015, the government invited organizations to bid for Thilafushi's management.

A $6/tourist green tax has also been proposed to fund a better solution here. Secure Bag is one company that has succeeded. At an investment of $1.5 million it has exported over 22,000 tonnes of iron scrap since 2008. Malé's fish market dumps 8–12 tonnes daily into the neighbourhood trashcan: the ocean. Rich in methane and carbon dioxide, this is a renewable energy source with massive bio fuel, organic fertilizer or compost potential.

Despite its solar power potential, the country runs almost entirely on diesel, spending over a quarter of its GDP on fuel. Temperatures hover within 27–32°C. The Maldives' first fully solar-powered resort launched in January 2015, with 6.5 km^2 of solar panels capable of producing 1,100 kW at peak. Dhiraagu, the nation's largest telecom provider, has installed solar power systems in 58 islands, covering over 1.5 km^2 across the country and producing 228,000 kWh annually. Another resort launched a floating 200 kWh solar power platform this summer.

Perhaps the most tragic irony is the widespread local apathy. Environmental preservation education is direly lacking. While local litter trends are preventable, currently they contribute significantly to the waste management nightmare. Travel is expensive – many locals see only a couple of islands and environmental challenges are thus out of sight and out of mind.

Approximately 25% of the population is unemployed. Expatriates (40,000 from Bangladesh alone) perform much of the unskilled, lower-paying or tougher work – jobs that could include locals, if only they were willing to perform them. One in three of the youth population engage in drug abuse. 30 gangs operate with about 10,000 members in Maldives. Given this *laissez-faire* attitude, experts predict that many residents may choose environmental refugee status instead of confronting these rising waters.

A silent absorber for centuries, the ocean can lash out. In 1987, exceptionally high tides swept over the country, inundating Malé. The 1998 El Niño killed 95% of the corals in Maldives. The 2004 Asian tsunami hit 69 islands, killing 82 people, displacing 30,000 and causing $472 million in damages – 62% of the nation's modest GDP.

Trends

The fact that Housing and Environment are under one Ministry is a telling fact of this nation's liveable-land dynamics. Also managed by this Ministry, the Baa Atoll became a UNESCO Biosphere Reserve in 2011, encompassing 75 islands, including 13 islands with 12,000 inhabitants. Six of the islands are also developed as resorts with over 350,000 tourists annually. The designation recognizes Baa Atoll's 140,000 ha area as a successful nexus of conservation, research and development that integrates biological and cultural diversity, combining core protected areas with sustainable development zones.

The government has set the target for the entire country to become a biosphere reserve by 2017. That's looking tough, given persisting practices such as dredging, land reclamation, sand collection and dumping in the sea. In spite of global reports predicting an expiry-date for this nation – inundation by 2100 for instance – it is empowering to realize that local living *can* improve. While more industrialized nations are responsible for rising sea levels, the local government and citizens can take meaningful measures to improve public living.

A significant part of the tourism market requires experiences that complement natural beauty and communities. This drives an economically promising triple-bottom-line business case: building considerate tourism that preserves island culture and biodiversity, both unique and sensitive to external and internal pressures. The company Greenpath, for instance, supplies environmentally friendly cleaning products. As another example, despite the humid climate, Reethi Beach Resort has successfully managed 100% natural mosquito control since 2011. Instead of highly toxic and ineffective daily pesticide fogging, the resort uses organic neem oil-based preventive measures.

Government policies

In 2009, Maldives pledged national carbon neutrality. Second only to Norway, Maldives' ten-year plan is more ambitious, aiming to totally decarbonize the local economy. In 2010, Maldives became the second country to ban shark fishing outright.

It may seem that, given their economic weight, resorts are largely left to their own devices. However, the 2005 development concept for resorts is pursued, backed by regulations. For instance, the plan requires that: environmental impact assessments be approved before development; buildings occupy under 20% of the land area; building heights not exceed tree tops; and coastal vegetation be maintained. With such measures, Maldives has become a successful trendsetter for relatively sustainable tourism development in Small Island Developing States (SIDS).

General regulations exist for environmental conservation and employment. Enforcement across Maldives' one-island-one-resort policy can be challenging, so the policies can be perceived more as recommendations. Transparency and governance requirements are also nascent in their development.

Case studies

Maldives Whale Shark Research Programme (MWSRP)

A research-based charity, MWSRP studies whale sharks and supports community-focused conservation initiatives fostering atoll-wide ecological, cultural and economic initiatives. MWSRP identified 260 sharks, recording 3,000 encounters in South Ari Atoll since 2006. Leveraging scientific data to advocate for conservation policy, MWSRP's findings contributed to the declaration of the 42 km² South Ari Marine Protected Area in 2009. Here, 78,000 tourists are involved in whale shark excursions annually, spending $9.4 million in 2013 (Cagua *et al.*, 2014).

In 2014, MWSRP became self-sufficient, thanks in part to visitors who pay for their volunteer research experience. Founded by foreign professionals, MWSRP aims to be Maldivian-run. It hosts month-long internships for Maldives National University students, and offers six-month apprenticeships for young Maldivians. MWSRP now has two full-time Maldivian managers.

Reefscapers

Since 2007, Reefscapers has combined coral propagation with a sponsorship programme to provide new habitats for marine life by increasing coral cover. By creating a literal sense of ownership, the target is that sponsors will not support activities contributing to degradation of their $150–500 "investment". Investors can monitor their coral frames' development online, receiving biannual photographic updates. Coral fragments are attached to locally made, rebar frames. Their construction provides alternative annual livelihoods of $55,000 to 15 local staff, partially offsetting the need to generate income from practices such as fishing. Marine biologists also educate local and international visitors about the extreme pressures corals face and their drastic decline. One of many such coral rehabilitation programmes, the Four Seasons Reefscapers programme, has placed 4,172 coral frames into local lagoons, growing 254,000 coral colonies, across 5,200 m^2. Sponsors and the resort have invested $965,000 over 7.5 years.

Shangri-La Villingili Resort

Shangri-La's Villingili Resort partnered with 140 local farmers to establish the Addu Meedhoo Cooperative Society (AMCS). Shangri-La purchases up to 80% of the produce from AMCS: over 233,000 kg to date. This is no small feat given that the saline coral sand is the only land available and most produce is imported. Farmers annually earn $1,500 this way. 60 have the potential to earn over $1,000/month. The resort includes local housewives in its supply chain. Daily, 20 women create 70 local flower welcome bouquets, collectively earning $14,400 annually. For supplying "short eats", local tea snacks, Shangri-La pays another $23,000 annually to local households. Shangri-La employs 60% Maldivians. Their 600-strong workforce includes differently abled employees.

Soneva Fushi Resort

At Soneva Fushi's waste management centre, Eco Centro, waste is wealth. All of the organic waste is composted into direly needed soil for its vegetable garden – annually producing 12,000 kg. In addition to its environmental benefits, this saves $100,000. With no food waste dumped in the ocean, Soneva produced enough compost to export to other islands this year. Overall, 81% of solid waste is recycled, including charcoal-making and reusing packing Styrofoam, for example as insulation in building walls or kickboards used to teach local children swimming. Soneva Fushi has practically eliminated plastic waste. Water is bottled in reusable glass bottles and room amenities in reusable ceramic containers. That's 100,000 fewer plastic bottles every year!

Further resources

About 500 NGOs are active here – while over 1,850 NGOs are registered. In addition to local environmental non-profit organizations such as Blue Peace, Manta Trust or the Ministry of Housing and Environment, global environmental organizations are active in Maldives too. Many resorts have also co-founded NGOs, such as Reethi Beach Resort's BAARU.

References

Cagua, E.F., Collins, N., Hancock, J. & Rees, R. (2014). Whale shark economics: a valuation of wildlife tourism in South Ari Atoll, Maldives. PeerJ 2:e515 http://dx.doi.org/10.7717/peerj.515.

Acknowledgements

The author would like to offer special thanks to her associates Naveen Balkhi, Mehr Fatima and Iselle McCalman.

11
Myanmar

Tapan Sarker
Discipline Leader, Sustainable Enterprise, Griffith University Business School, Australia

Swe Sett Kyu Pe
School of Engineering, Griffith University, Australia

National context

Myanmar is the second largest country in South-East Asia and has a total land area of 676,577 km^2. It borders five nations – Bangladesh, India, China, Laos and Thailand – with over 2,800 km of coastline. It is a nation with a tiny population of 60 million compared with the massive populations of its rapidly growing neighbours – China and India.

Rich in natural resources, Myanmar has the potential for economic growth as it attracts foreign investments. From the late 1940s to late 1960s, Myanmar was a leading regional economy and a major exporter of rice in the world market. However, the country's growth rate was negatively affected by the flawed policies of the government at that time, and poor management.

From 1962 to 1988 the country was under military rule and the Burmese Way of Socialism was introduced. As a result of the control-oriented economy under this Socialist government, the economic situation worsened. After 1988, the Military Junta took power and the market-oriented economy was introduced, although economic mismanagement and corruption have continued to cripple the country's economy.

After the election in 2010, a new quasi-civilian government came into power and a series of political and economic reforms were introduced. The USA and EU have lifted economic sanctions and these recent reforms are encouraging foreign investment. The current GDP of $43 billion is expected to increase by 6% annually until 2020.

Priority issues

Recent political changes in Myanmar have institutionalized a more democratic system of governance and paved the way for the economy (Chalk, 2013). With a wealth of assets, Myanmar is well-positioned for a multipronged development strategy that draws on agriculture, mining and extraction, manufacturing, and services (OECD, 2013). The current economic outlook is favourable with a projected GDP growth rate of 7.5% in 2013/14 and 7.75% in 2014/15 (IMF, 2014).

Despite the growth rate, Myanmar faces various challenges. The lack of infrastructural development is the main concern for foreign investors. For example, road density is very low with only 21% of roads paved (OECD, 2013). Myanmar's per capita electricity consumption is the lowest among the Association of South-East Asian Nations (ASEAN) countries and 70% of the population do not have access to reliable power supplies. Myanmar also has the lowest mobile phone user penetration rate in South-East Asia at 9% (KPMG, 2013).

The lack of skilled workers and professionals is another challenge. A strong focus on vocational training and the cultivation of a higher proportion of tertiary graduates are essential, since sustainable development is conditional on the availability and quality of human capital (OECD, 2013).

Another urgent priority is creating robust legal and institutional structures for businesses. The Ministry of National Planning and Economic Development is responsible for enterprise registration and administration but has not captured the statistics of the business community. As a consequence of this, various governmental committees have been established to coordinate issues related to industries and sectors, creating great inefficiency (OECD, 2013). The right institutional framework for entrepreneurship initiatives would allow the business sector to become a driving force for development.

Trends

Social and sustainable enterprises are new in Myanmar and few organizations identify themselves as such. Recognized social enterprises are registered as private limited companies or cooperatives. They aim to balance their social mission and core business to achieve a financially sustainable social impact.

Some corporations and businesses have created foundations and engaged with charities. Although most foundations are not financially sustainable, they have corporate funding and could help the development of the social enterprise sector.

In Myanmar, most of the social enterprises focus on five types of socially beneficial service:

- **Provision of basic services** – Supplying basic healthcare and education to disadvantaged populations

- **Civic engagement and civil society promotion** – Research, publication and training on environmental sustainability and social entrepreneurship

- **Targeted livelihood enhancement programmes** – Microloans and revolving funds for sustainable forestry or vocational training

- **Access to finance** – Microfinance services allowing organizations to grow their businesses and generate revenue

- **Provision of socially beneficial products and services** – Supplying mosquito nets, water pumps and water filters to disadvantaged populations

Local entrepreneurs run the social enterprises as they understand local needs. The mature social enterprises and organizations balance relationships with authorities and focus on social impact, including livelihood programmes in agricultural communities. Successful sustainable and social enterprises focus on capacity building and training for their staff.

However, there are challenges and constraints such as under-developed human capital, lack of access to financial capital and basic physical infrastructure, poor supply of goods and high rental costs for real estate.

Government policies

Prior to 2013, Myanmar was rated as one of the worst business climates in the world due to political instability, macroeconomic mismanagement, inadequate infrastructure, an unreliable banking system, poor education system and administrative obstacles (Rieffel, 2012). Since then, a series of reforms have been undertaken, such the launch of a 20-year National Comprehensive Development Plan (NCDP) with four five-year programmes to raise living standards and increase development.

The framework for Economic and Social Reform (FESR) outlines Myanmar's policies towards achieving NCDP's long-term goals. Under this framework the government has identified priorities for sustained industrial development to catch up with global economies while maintaining agricultural reforms, poverty alleviation and rural development (KPMG, 2013).

The government recognizes the potential of the agriculture sector and stimulating wider rural development to achieve growth and poverty reduction. It is also conscious that low productivity, poor marketing, lack of access to quality research and inadequate support for the farming community have limited the growth in the sector.

Policies, laws and regulations to support small and medium-sized enterprises (SMEs) have been reviewed to address past difficulties. The policies proposed for development of SMEs include one-stop centres for business start-ups, reducing and eliminating administrative controls, supporting provision of land-use rights and building enterprise capacity, including access to finance and markets. The government also proposes to encourage the development of micro-enterprises as well as microfinance institutions (Government of Myanmar, 2013).

Case studies

Forest Resources Environment Development and Conservation Association (FREDA)

FREDA is a non-political, non-profit non-governmental organization working in the forestry sector in Myanmar. Founded in 1996, the organization has more than 500 members comprising academics from various fields such as forestry, botany, zoology, veterinary sciences, hydrogeology, as well as people with business, journalism and arts backgrounds. FREDA's objectives are to promote participation and partnership in sustainable forest management, natural environment conservation, wildlife protection, grass-roots-level community development, human resource development, disaster risk reduction, sustainable land use and responsible eco-tourism.

FREDA has been engaged in community development, recognizing the need for the sustainable development of rural communities and conservation of the environment. In collaboration with international NGOs, FREDA provides appropriate agro-forestry technology for the growing of leguminous plants for fodder and fruit trees in rural farming communities to generate sustainable revenues. These activities have been ongoing since 1998 in the Peyintaung village tract of Kalaw Township in Southern Shan State and have shown increases in the productivity and sustainable development of the rural community.

FREDA is also currently involved in a mangrove reforestation project in the Ayeyarwady Delta where natural mangrove forests were depleted due to encroachment by rice farmers. The mangrove forests are required to protect the rice fields from the extrusion of salt water and acid sulphates. Many farmers have abandoned the rice fields as their farms became less productive after years of encroaching mangroves. Since 1999, FREDA has distributed mangrove seedlings to the local community to be planted.

Apart from mangroves reforestation, FREDA is also involved in watershed management and wildlife protection programmes, as well as supporting outstanding scholars at local universities for further studies in various fields such as botany, biology, ecology, environmental science, forestry and zoology.

Proximity Design

Proximity Design is one of the largest non-profit social enterprises operating in Myanmar, working to help reduce poverty for rural families in a sustainable and effective way. Proximity Design was established in 2004 and promotes products and services to low-income farmers that enable them to increase their income.

For example, working with a group of designers and engineers, Proximity Design engineered irrigation products for farming communities. In 2012, the organization also launched sales of solar lights, providing a cheap and sustainable lighting option in rural areas. Since its establishment, 110,000 products have been sold to farm households in Myanmar, improving lifestyles and boosting incomes for over 250,000 rural people.

Proximity Design also launched farm advisory services in 2008, which provide training for 35,000 farmers in the Ayeyarwady Delta region to increase yields and improve crop health. Financial services are provided to address the lack of formalized banking systems and limited microfinance options in some rural areas. In 2013, the organization extended 10,014 agricultural loans to small-plot rice farmers in the Ayeyarwady Delta region.

Since 2010, Proximity Design has funded 546 community-managed rural infrastructure projects in over 400 villages in the country, with most located in the central Dry Zone and Ayeyarwady Delta regions. Projects in the Dry Zone are related to rainwater harvesting reservoirs, while in the Ayeyarwady Delta region, projects focus on building footpaths for easier and quicker access to schools, hospitals and market towns, as well as building jetties to allow larger boats to dock near remote villages, thus opening up trade opportunities for the local community. Proximity Design allows villagers to participate in the construction of local projects in different ways and villagers receive daily wages.

Yangon Bakehouse

Yangon Bakehouse is a social business dedicated to providing disadvantaged groups in Myanmar with job skills and experience. It also provides life skills training and employment opportunities for women. Yangon Bakehouse provides a fair wage, work skills training, medical benefits, life skill courses and career assistance after completion of the programme. They also promote sustainability by connecting with like-minded suppliers, small farmers and growers that use sustainable practices. The Bakehouse is financed by small grants from local corporate sponsors and foundations that focus on building up women's economic power and education. Yangon Bakehouse has been established for two years and so far about 35 women have been trained.

Further resources

Asian Development Bank (ADB) – Resumed operations in Myanmar in 2013 with an assistance package for social and economic development. ADB promotes sustainable and inclusive economic development and job creation in the support of poverty reduction.

Ayeyarwady Foundation – A non-profit organization established by the Max Myanmar group of companies and actively taking part in religious, social, education and health activities.

Htoo Foundation – Established by the Htoo Group of companies and supporting health, education, culture, regional development and preservation of the national habitat, as well as offering emergency assistance after natural disasters.

Pact Myanmar – An international NGO that implements projects on health and livelihood, community development, microfinance and food security.

Opportunities Now – An entrepreneurship training school which seeks to reduce poverty by providing business training and mentoring in various stages of business start-up.

References

Chalk, P. (2013). On the path of change: political, economic and social challenges for Myanmar. Australian Strategic Policy Institute, Special Report, December.

Government of Myanmar (2013). Republic of the Union of Myanmar – Millennium Development Goals Report. Naypyidaw: Government of Myanmar.

IMF (2014). Myanmar: IMF completes second review of Staff Monitored Program. Washington, DC: International Monetary Fund.

KPMG (2013). Infrastructure in Myanmar. New York: KPMG.

OECD (2013). Structural policy country notes – Myanmar. Paris: OECD.

Rieffel, L. (2012). Myanmar economy: tough choices. Brookings, Global Economy & Development Working Paper, September 2012.

12
New Zealand

Christopher Fleming
Associate Professor, Department of Accounting, Finance and Economics, and Asia–Pacific Centre for Sustainable Enterprise, Griffith University, Australia

Matthew Manning
Senior Lecturer, Centre for Aboriginal Economic Policy Research, The Australian National University, Australia

National context

New Zealand (Aotearoa) is an island nation situated in the south-western Pacific Ocean approximately 2,000 km east of Australia. New Zealand consists of two main islands (the North Island or Te Ika-a-Māui and the South Island or Te Waipounamu) as well as a number of small outlying islands. In 2013, New Zealand had a population of 4.5 million. Approximately 69% of the New Zealand population are of European descent. The native Māori people represent the largest minority (14.6%), followed by Asians (9.2%) and non-Māori Pacific Islanders (6.9%). There are two official languages: English and Māori. Just over half of the population identify themselves as Christians, while just over one-third of the population report having no religion (Pew Research Center, 2012).

In 2013 New Zealand's Gross Domestic Product (GDP) was US$185.8 billion, corresponding to a per capita figure of $41,555. This places New Zealand in the "high-income" category. Recent economic growth has been moderate, with per capita GDP growth in 2013 of 1.6%, and an average growth rate between 2000 and 2013 of 1.4% per annum (World Bank, 2014).

According to the 2014 United Nations' Human Development Index (HDI), New Zealand ranked seventh out of 187 countries, with a score of 0.910. This places New Zealand in the "very high" human development category. Between 1980 and 2013, New Zealand's HDI value increased from 0.793 to 0.910, an increase of 14.8%. This HDI score is above the OECD average (0.876) and also above the average of countries in the very high development group (0.890) (United Nations Development Programme, 2014).

Priority issues

New Zealand performs very well across a number of domains, including economic performance, social cohesiveness, gender equality and population health. Nonetheless, at least two significant challenges remain; environmental degradation and the socioeconomic gap between Māori and non-Māori.

With regard to the environment, New Zealand has approximately 14 million ha (around half) of its original native vegetation. Approximately 8.2 million ha are legally protected, with the remaining 5.8 million ha having no formal protection. Of the unprotected areas, approximately 468,000 ha is of land environments reduced to less than 20% of their original extent. This is of concern as the rate of biodiversity loss increases dramatically when native vegetation cover drops below 20% (Ministry for the Environment, 2007).

Some environments have suffered greater reductions in extent than others. For example, human activity has reduced the remaining wetlands in New Zealand to less than 9.4% (approximately 45,600 ha) of their original extent. This is of concern as at least 20% of vascular (sappy) plant species depend on short-lived (ephemeral) wetlands that occupy less than 1% of the country's land area. Similarly, only 11.6% (approximately 21,300 ha) of New Zealand's original dunelands remain (Ministry for the Environment, 2007).

With regard to the socioeconomic status of Māori and non-Māori populations, despite significant policy efforts and substantial investment, persistent gaps remain. For example, Māori life expectancy is approximately 7.3 years lower than non-Māori, although the gap is closing (Statistics New Zealand, 2013b). Māori are overrepresented in the New Zealand corrections system; representing approximately 15% of the general population, Māori make up 51% of the prison population (Department of Corrections, 2014).

In 2013, the median weekly income of Māori persons aged 15 years and over was NZ$486 (US$374), compared with a figure of NZ$575 (US$443) for the population as a whole. In part this reflects an unemployment rate that is over twice that of the national average (6.0% compared with 12.8%) (Statistics New Zealand, 2013a, 2013c).

Trends

The Sustainable Business Council of New Zealand is the primary source of information on the states and trends of sustainable enterprise. Since 2009 the Council has conducted an annual survey of business and consumer behaviour. The most recent (2013) survey of 2,152 respondents confirms an accelerating decline in organizations engaged in sustainable business practices in New Zealand (Horizon Research, 2013).

For example, the proportion of organizations that respond positively to the statement "actively purchases goods and services from suppliers who act sustainably" has fallen from 26% in 2009 to 19.3% in 2013. Similarly, in response to the question, "Does the organization you work for (or with) have a sustainable development strategy?" the proportion of respondents who answered "yes" has fallen from 38.7% in 2009 to 27.4% in 2013. In response to the question, "Would you say your organization behaves sustainably (looks after profits as well as the environment and people)?" the proportion of respondents who answered "yes" has fallen from 60% in 2009 to 53% in 2013.

In contrast to the decline in sustainable practice by organizations, the survey finds a re-emergence (from the previous year's survey) of consumer support for organizations that behave sustainably. For example, in response to the question, "Do you personally consider sustainable factors when purchasing goods or services for yourself, your family or your organization?" the proportion answering "yes, all of the time" or "yes, some of the time" has risen from 80.3% in 2012 to 82% in 2013. Similarly, in response to the question, "Would you switch to another brand of product or service if you found your regular brand or service provider was having a bad effect on the environment, people or society, or behaving unethically?" the proportion answering "yes" has risen from 61.7% in 2012 to 66.8% in 2013.

Government policies

The New Zealand Government has recently introduced a number of initiatives to support sustainable and innovative enterprise. For example, in February 2013 Callaghan Innovation was established as a stand-alone Crown Entity. Made up of a team of about 400 researchers, scientists, engineers, technologists, business people, investment managers and account managers, the Entity aims to give businesses a "single front door" to the innovation system, and accelerate commercialization of innovation by New Zealand firms. Callaghan Innovation offers expertise and facilities, operates its own research and technology laboratories, and manages more than NZ$140 million (US$108 million) per annum in government funding and grants to support business innovation and capability building.

Another relatively recent innovation is the establishment of a Small Business Development Group. Made up entirely of small business owners, the purpose of this group is to advise government on issues affecting small and medium-sized enterprises (SMEs) and to give SMEs more say in policy development. The overarching objective is to promote growth in the SME sector.

Further, the New Zealand Government has developed a range of resources to assist organizations in adopting sustainable enterprise practices, including Envirostep, carboNZero and EECA Business (see under "Further resources").

The Resource Management Act 1991 (RMA) is the principal means through which the environmental impacts of economic activities are managed in New Zealand. The core purpose of the Act is to promote the sustainable management of natural and physical resources by safeguarding the life-supporting capacity of air, water, soil and ecosystems. There are a number of national environmental standards under sections 43 and 44 of the Act, relating to noise, contaminants, water quality, air quality and monitoring.

Case studies

Penguin Place Conservation Reserve

Located on the Otago Peninsula of New Zealand's South Island, Penguin Place is a private conservation reserve dedicated to protecting the Yellow

Eyed Penguin (*Megadyptes antipodes*). Founded by Howard McGrouther in 1985, the reserve is entirely funded by guided tours. This funding provides habitat restoration, predator control, a research programme and on-site rehabilitation care. The reserve is part of a working sheep farm and the owners aim to create as many breeding opportunities for the penguins as possible, while minimizing the loss of productive farmland. Since the early 1990s the conservation reserve has funded a rigorous scientific research and monitoring programme. Ongoing trapping, shooting and poisoning efforts are undertaken to protect the penguins and native birds from predation by introduced mammals.

Phoenix Organics

Established in 1986, Phoenix Organics is a soft drinks company that has a vision to create a business that is good for the planet and great for health and wellbeing. In a competitive market dominated by large multinational corporations, Phoenix Organics has successfully attempted to provide an alternative product, with no preservatives or artificial ingredients. Phoenix is now the most widely distributed premium beverage brand in New Zealand. Originally focusing on using natural products and organic ingredients wherever possible, in 1999 the company committed to becoming 100% organic. All products offered by Phoenix Organics, with the exception of their hot beverage range, are now certified organic (as at 2014). The company is strongly supportive of New Zealand remaining free of genetically engineered crops and believes New Zealand should continue to build on its "clean green image".

Whale Watch

Whale Watch is a multiple award-winning New Zealand nature tourism company, owned and operated by the Indigenous Kati Kuri people of Kaikoura, a Māori subtribe of the South Island's larger Ngai Tahu Tribe. Whale Watch was founded in 1987 during a period of significant economic decline in New Zealand. The company has helped Kaikoura to become one of New Zealand's leading tourism destinations, stimulating investment in tourism infrastructure throughout the seaside settlement. Having spent more than ten years working towards improving its sustainability goals, the town of Kaikoura recently became the first community in the Southern Hemisphere to gain Earthcheck Platinum certification. Earthcheck is the world's leading environmental benchmarking and certification programme for the travel and tourism industry. Since its inception, Whale Watch has been the recipient of many awards, including the Pacific Asia Travel Association Gold Award, the World Travel and Tourism Council Tourism for Tomorrow Community Benefit Award, and the Pacific Asia Travel Association Gold Award in the Culture and Heritage category.

Further resources

carboNZero – A programme, managed by Landcare Research New Zealand Limited, which provides New Zealand businesses with an ISO 14065 greenhouse gas certification. This requires businesses to scientifically measure their carbon footprint and develop a business-wide plan for systematic emissions reduction.

EECA – The Energy Efficiency and Conservation Authority aims to support and promote energy efficiency, conservation and the use of renewable sources of energy in New Zealand to both consumers and businesses. EECA offers a variety of support to small businesses – from practical advice and mentoring, through to funding and awarding grants.

Envirostep – A free self-assessment tool developed by the Ministry of Economic Development to help organizations to understand, improve and communicate their environmental performance.

Parliamentary Commissioner for the Environment – Set up under the Environment Act 1986, the Parliamentary Commissioner for the Environment is an independent Officer of Parliament with wide-ranging powers to investigate environmental concerns. The Commissioner is independent in that he/she does not report to a Government Minister, but to Parliament through either the Speaker of the House or the Officers of Parliament Committee.

Sustainable Business Council of New Zealand – This organization aims to contribute towards achieving a sustainable New Zealand and global sustainable development. The Council currently has 66 members, including some of New Zealand's largest and most well-known companies.

References

Department of Corrections (2014). Prison facts and statistics – March 2014. Auckland: Government of New Zealand.

Horizon Research (2013). Business and consumer behaviour 2013. Auckland: Horizon Research.

Ministry for the Environment (2007). Protecting Our Places: Introducing the National Priorities for Protecting Rare and Threatened Native Biodiversity on Private Land. Wellington: Government of New Zealand.

Pew Research Center (2012). Religious Composition by Country. Washington, DC: Pew Resesarch Center.

Statistics New Zealand (2013a). Household Labour Force Survey: December 2013 Quarter. Auckland: Government of New Zealand.

Statistics New Zealand (2013b). Narrowing gap between Māori and non-Māori life expectancy Christchurch. Auckland: Government of New Zealand.

Statistics New Zealand (2013c). New Zealand income survey: June 2013 Quarter. Auckland: Government of New Zealand.

United Nations Development Programme (2014). Explanatory note on the 2014 Human Development Report Composite Indices – New Zealand. New York: UNDP.

World Bank (2014). Data – New Zealand. Washington, DC: World Bank.

13
Norfolk Island

Arunima Malik
ISA, School of Physics, The University of Sydney, Australia
Denise Quintal
EcoNorfolk Foundation Inc Limited, Norfolk Island

Background

Norfolk Island is located in the Pacific Ocean and lies between Australia, New Zealand and New Caledonia. It is approximately 1,670 km east-north-east of Sydney and has a total area of 35 km². The island includes two small uninhabited islands – Nepean and Phillip. Norfolk Island is well known for its rich history. It was "discovered" in 1774 by a British explorer, navigator and cartographer, Captain James Cook.

Prior to his discovery, the island is thought to have been occupied by East Polynesian seafarers in the 14th or 15th century. However, at the time of Cook's arrival, the island was uninhabited, and remained so for a further 14 years until the Australian convict settlements between 1788 and 1855. In 1856, Norfolk Island was resettled by the descendants of Bounty mutineers and Tahitians from Pitcairn Island. However, some Pitcairn Island descendants did not like Norfolk Island, and returned back to Pitcairn Island where their ancestors reside today.

Norfolk Island is a self-governing territory of Australia under the Norfolk Island Act 1979 (COA, 2013). The Act limits the level of involvement of the Commonwealth of Australia in the island's administrative and government matters. Under the Act, the Legislative Assembly of Norfolk Island is entitled to pass and implement laws independently of the Australian Government, except for the acquisition of property on other than just terms, the raising of defence forces, the coining of money and euthanasia. Norfolk Island does not follow the Australian taxation, social security or welfare systems.

The island receives significant funding from the Commonwealth. Over a number of years the Commonwealth has provided many millions of dollars to make sure that the essential services are functioning and the World Heritage site of Kingston and Arthurs Vale Historic Area (KAVHA) is maintained. Since 2010–11 a total of $33 million has been provided to the Administration of Norfolk Island (ANI) for meeting ongoing and emergency funding obligations (ANI, 2013).

Norfolk Island's main economic activity is tourism. During the early 2000s, the island experienced an influx of visitors in the order of 40,000 per year. However, the industry has seen a steady decline in tourist numbers, with only 22,400 visiting the island in 2012–13 (ANI, 2013). Due to a decline in tourists, the Norfolk Island economy is facing an economic and financial recession. This downturn compromises the ability of the government to undertake crucial infrastructure upgrades and implement renewable energy technologies for addressing the energy and waste management issues.

Priority issues

Small islands such as Norfolk face significant energy and waste issues. Norfolk Island depends on imported diesel for running its primary electricity producing power plant. The cost of imported fuel determines the cost of electricity on the island. The freight costs of shipping diesel to Norfolk Island are high. As a result, Norfolk Islanders have to pay three times the amount of money paid by mainland Australians for their electricity usage (ACIL Tasman, 2012).

The electricity on the island is produced from diesel, which produces greenhouse gas emissions. Norfolk Island receives sunshine throughout the year, an average of seven hours per day (ANI, 2013). Therefore, solar photovoltaic electricity generation is the most feasible option on the island. However, solar panels are expensive to install and maintain. Implementation of solar energy or other renewable energy technology requires significant amounts of funds that are unavailable due to the Norfolk Island Government's poor fiscal position (ACIL Tasman, 2012).

In addition to energy, Norfolk Island – just like any other Pacific island – faces the issue of waste management and disposal. At Norfolk Island, waste is collected and managed by the ANI at the Waste Management Centre. Residents are required to bring their waste to the centre, which is then collected and transported to a cliff at Headstone. The waste is then burned, and the residue dumped into the ocean.

The dumping of residual waste results in water pollution that threatens marine life around the island. To deal with this issue of waste management, monetary investment is needed to bring the waste management system up to the standards of mainland Australia. However, due to economic depression, the Norfolk Island government does not have the financial resources needed to upgrade the waste management facility.

To deal with the high cost of energy and waste disposal, Norfolk islanders have devised ingenious solutions for tackling these issues by recycling and reusing existing resources, as showcased in the next section.

Trends

In collaboration with the University of Sydney, EcoNorfolk foundation has successfully undertaken comprehensive triple-bottom-line (TBL) foot-printing studies for several businesses around the island. The TBL analysis allows the local businesses to get an overview of their overall performance, and assess ways to reduce their costs and environmental impacts. The findings from one such case study (Lenzen, 2008) are described in the next section.

Case studies

Cascade Soft Drink Factory

The Cascade Soft Drink Factory on Norfolk Island is a good example of material recycling and reuse. The factory is the primary producer of carbonated soft drinks on the island. The owner of the factory has put in place measures for reducing the factory's material, energy, carbon and water usage. The products from the factory are sold in glass bottles that are recycled. The industry produces little or no waste because reusable plastic crates are used for distributing the products, bottles are reused after washing and sterilizing, and broken and unusable bottles are crushed and used as road fill.

The factory has a rainwater tank for harvesting rainwater. The rainwater is purified and used for washing and sterilizing glass bottles. Use of rainwater greatly reduces the amount of water extracted from the ground – thus reducing the overall water usage. The owner of the factory has also employed thermal insulation for reducing the overall energy use. The cool storage room is well insulated with foam to reduce the electricity consumption. Reduction in energy use has allowed the enterprise to reduce its greenhouse gas emissions as well.

The triple-bottom-line analysis reveals that the factory performs better than other soft drink industries (Lenzen, 2008) in terms of environmental impacts. The Cascade Soft Drink industry's material, energy, carbon, water and land disturbance footprints are all lower than an average soft drink producer (Lenzen, 2008).

Point Howe Pig Farm

Another example of a sustainable enterprise is the pig farm at Point Howe in Norfolk Island. The farm is the primary supplier of meat products, such as bacon and ham, to the island community. When the farm was first established in 1976, the owner realized that a major issue with pig farming is the tonnes of pig effluent produced each day. Ineffective disposal of pig effluent causes surface and groundwater contamination. To deal with this waste issue, the owner has established an anaerobic digestion infrastructure on his farm to extract biogas from pig effluent. Anaerobic digestion is a proven technique for managing waste to produce energy. The use of pig effluent for producing biogas greatly reduces water and air pollution, thereby maintaining environmental quality and promoting sustainable development. The biogas is used for heating and cooking food.

In addition to supplying bacon and ham, the farm also produces fresh fruits and vegetables. The solid component left after extracting the biogas from the manure is used as a fertilizer for the soil. This enterprise is a clear example of making the island self-sufficient to reduce the amount of food imports into the island, and to produce fresh meat, fruits and vegetables on the farm. In terms of sustainability performance, the farm's greenhouse gas emissions, water use, material flow and land disturbance are lower than an average pig farm (Lenzen, 2008).

Sustainable Islands Project

One programme that the EcoNorfolk Foundation (ENF) is involved in is the Sustainable Islands Workshops, organized in partnership with the University of Sydney. The Department of Foreign Affairs and Trade (DFAT), Commonwealth of Australia (previously AusAid) has funded the workshop and project. The aim of the project is to exchange ideas and skills between different Pacific Islands, and discuss ways of dealing with the energy and waste issues that all Pacific Islands face. Furthermore, the programme allows the Norfolk Island community to showcase their sustainable businesses. Outcomes of the workshops have seen networks with other pacific islands such as Rarotonga and Norfolk Island commence.

In mid-2014, the founder of ENF visited Rarotonga, and signed a Memorandum of Understanding with Titikaveka Oire Inc. group at the Titikaveka Community Centre, Rarotonga, Cook Islands. The aim is to work at advancing the science of sustainability in their community. The village has 1,500 residents and they are struggling with their piggeries. They are keen to copy Farmer Lou by using the same principles as the methane digester on Norfolk Island. This will eventually open up opportunities for the other islands within the Cook Islands cluster to undertake such steps towards achieving sustainability.

Further resources

EcoNorfolk Foundation – To motivate the local residents to support sustainable development, a non-profit organization – EcoNorfolk Foundation – hosts public campaigns and workshops around the island. The workshops are designed to educate the local community about promoting the science of sustainability by preserving the island's natural heritage and resources. In addition to promoting sustainability on Norfolk Island, the EcoNorfolk Foundation also organizes events and programmes for officials from other Pacific Islands to promote interisland environmental awareness. By lobbying local and also the Australian Governments, and informing the local people through the media, most islanders appear to be knowledgeable and have an understanding of preservation and sustainability.

References

ACIL Tasman (2012). Norfolk Island Economic Development Report: Reform of the Norfolk Island Economy. Department of Regional Australia, Regional Development and Local Government. Canberra.

ANI (2013). Norfolk Island Annual Report 2012–2013. Kingston, Norfolk Island.

COA (2013). Norfolk Island Act 1979. Canberra: Commonwealth of Australia.

Lenzen, M. (2008). Sustainable island businesses: a case study of Norfolk Island. *Journal of Cleaner Production*, 16, 2018–2035.

14
Pakistan

Akash Ghai
Co-Founder, Development Three, USA

Muneezay Jaffery
Operations Manager, Green Shoots Foundation, UK

National context

Pakistan – which shares borders with Afghanistan, China, India and Iran – has an area of 796,095 km^2 and had an estimated population of 184 million in 2012/13 (UNDP, 2013). Islam is the main religion in Pakistan accounting for around 98% of the population, with the remaining 2% predominantly Christian. Islamabad is the capital, while Karachi is the largest city. In 1947 Pakistan became independent from the British Indian Empire and has since become a major exporter of goods such as cotton, leather, rice and sporting goods.

Pakistan has adopted the Millennium Development Goals (MDGs) set out by the UNDP and while considerable progress has been made, significant gaps still exist for education, water and sanitation, shelter and personal rights (Social Progress Imperative, 2014). Despite some reluctance to adopt sustainable enterprise at both state and government level, urban areas such as Karachi and Lahore are starting to become hubs for social enterprises and innovators (Shah and Shubhisham, 2012).

Priority issues

In September 2013 the International Monetary Fund (IMF) warned that Pakistan was facing serious economic challenges that needed addressing. Stagnating national growth and an increasingly young population (63% of the population is aged 25 or under) make it difficult for the country to address its socioeconomic challenges, such as rural poverty, disease and illiteracy. This situation has been exacerbated by natural disasters in recent years, such as a major earthquake in 2005 and floods in 2010 and 2011.

The government faces ongoing civil unrest, rising security costs and extensive population displacement. The fight against the Taliban has not only put a significant economic strain on the country but has cost Pakistan socially, in terms of infrastructure and human capital. However, resolution to such matters is not easily achieved.

Another pressing issue concerns the role of Pakistani citizens and the global supply chain of the country. Poor labour and human rights practices have been uncovered within the textiles and sporting goods production sectors. In the late 1990s Pakistan produced 75% of the total world production of footballs, but what the world did not know was that most of the workforces were made up of children. In 2012 it was estimated that millions of children were engaged in child labour. It is believed that since then, this has decreased thanks to the government passing the Human Rights Act. This has led to greater access to education for children; however, more data is needed to fully assess the changes made in child labour practices.

While third sector and aid organizations can help to fill gaps left by the government, responsible business and social entrepreneurship alone cannot alleviate all the country's challenges. Despite these limitations, sustainable enterprise is growing in Pakistan as a way of achieving social and environmental impacts along with returns on investment.

Trends

The British Council, in collaboration with the YES Network Pakistan, profiles Pakistani social entrepreneurs in its report, Enterprising Pakistan (2013), many of whom are young entrepreneurs focused on creating positive impacts in the areas of environment, health and skills development. This suggests a growing desire among the entrepreneurs to adopt a hybrid profit-making and social development model. A parallel trend is towards the adoption of Corporate Social Responsibility (CSR). CSR is becoming the buzzword around meeting tables in Pakistan. It is slowly garnering public and media attention.

The traditional thought process is if companies do not assume social responsibility there is no expectation for it (CSR WeltWeit, 2012). As long as the healthcare and living expenses of employees are met through their salaries there are no further expectations of a company. But recent developments have challenged this thinking. In September 2014 the NGO, WWF-Pakistan, and Daraz.pk (an online Pakistan-based fashion retailer) signed an agreement to initiate the sale of WWF-Pakistan's Panda Products online. (Pakistan Observer, 2014) This cross-sector collaboration within the CSR sphere could become a future trend. Companies should see both the tangible and intangible benefits of pursuing such an agreement with emphasis on the social and ethical benefits, which can lead to sustainable growth and better outputs.

According to data from the Trade Development Authority of Pakistan (TDAP) there has been an increase in the value of commodities trading in the country from May 2013 to May 2014. Textiles and Clothing has a value increase of 11.26% and Agro Food has an increase of 17.06% (TDAP, 2014). This signifies that despite the issues identified previously, production is still going strong. These production and export sectors play a crucial role in shaping the future of the country. The question is now whether this trend will continue, particularly if the human rights and labour issues faced by the country are addressed and ethical practices are implemented resulting in output decline.

Research and Development (R&D) is crucial if Pakistan is to build on its growing product base. Unfortunately there is little investment in agriculture-based R&D. This is based on the fact that researchers and scientists focus in more mainstream industries such as oil and gas. One positive trend is that the "brain drain" – where highly educated and skilled citizens leave Pakistan due to lacking investment in R&D, economic opportunities, social security and technological infrastructure – appears to be reversing, with internationally educated Pakistanis moving back to cities such as Karachi and Lahore. This has been achieved partly by improving the lacking infrastructure and partly by appealing to Pakistanis' entrepreneurial natures.

To further enhance this move, the Ministry of Science and Technology implemented the Science, Technology and Innovation Policy in 2012. Bute

(2013) highlights that Pakistan is expected to increase its R&D expenditure by 1% of the national GDP by 2015 and 2% by 2020. The policy seeks to help contribute to the achievement of these targets by "promoting R&D activities, programmes for technology transfer and technology development". This is a way to encourage research enterprises and their employees to stay in country and contribute to the national "big picture".

In September 2014, Invest2Innovate (2014) issued the Pakistan Entrepreneurship Ecosystem Report 2014. The report highlights a significant increase in the number of "incubators, co-working spaces, and competitions in the last two years". This suggestion of actualized activities taking place to stimulate the start-up and small enterprise market is definitely a positive sign. From the concept stage through to the growth and investment stages more incubators, accelerators and funders are becoming accessible to individuals who have an idea. The report profiles four of the largest incubators in Pakistan with particular emphasis on the technology sector. Incubators like these give young talented individuals the opportunity to test their products and services before rolling them out city then nationwide.

Government policies

In order to develop sustainable enterprise in Pakistan, government support is crucial. There is little or no direct support for sustainable or social enterprises, although there has been some support for the CSR agenda (Shah and Shubhisham, 2012). For example, in 2013 the Securities and Exchange Commission of Pakistan (SECP) approved guidelines for CSR. These highlight the value of CSR and how companies can adjust their strategies to incorporate responsible actions. The next decade will test whether these CSR guidelines are implemented effectively.

The Economic Policy Group (EPG) suggests that the role of the government in supporting business school incubator hubs is vital. Incubator hubs assess all strands required to develop successful businesses from research to funding to start-up. The EPG believe that the Pakistani government should create policies that support the development of these hubs and provide resources necessary to help them grow, without interfering in their operations.

As mentioned, global production of footballs is predominantly central-ized in Pakistan, however, due to lacking technology China has quickly risen to lead global production. Yet for the 2014 Fifa World Cup, a firm in Sialkot (a city in the Punjab province) won the contract to produce the footballs. The Human Rights Act seeks to address the child labour practices at national level but the 2000 World Federation of Sporting Goods Industry Code of Conduct takes this to the international stage. This brings visibility to the standards the country must uphold in order to continue delivering a global product, which contributes much to the national output. International regulatory bodies like this determine whether Pakistani firms abide by clear ethical and social principles across a multitude of high-demand sectors.

Case studies

Buksh Foundation

As Pakistan is an Islamic nation, microfinance is sadly not a widely accepted concept, since most microfinance institutions (MFIs) do not comply with Islamic teachings and religious scripture. The Buksh Foundation has adopted the MFI model, and has begun to integrate aspects of CSR and social enterprise. The Foundation offers loans to micro-entrepreneurs to generate income and to create or sustain self-employment. One of its core focus areas is on energy needs in rural areas. In February 2014, Buksh partnered with Ufone to deliver an initiative that will provide targeted communities with solar lighting devices to replace polluting and unhealthy kerosene oil lamps. Buksh aims to provide Ufone with technical support, which gives Ufone a better foothold to drive this and any future CSR initi-atives. Despite Pakistan's reluctance to adopt MFI as a model for change, Buksh is a catalyst that is helping to challenge the mind-set of Pakistanis by showing the benefits of microfinance and its ability to help marginalized groups in the country.

Faraz Khan

Apart from organizations that support the sustainable enterprise agenda in Pakistan, there are also individuals such as Faraz Khan who are trying to deliver impact. Khan is a UK-based Pakistani social entrepreneur who established the SEED Ventures hub, among other sustainable enterprise focused organizations over the past ten years. With a banking background,

Khan sought to use his experience to foster the creation and development of social enterprises in both Pakistan and the UK. Khan is an example of individuals seeking to acquire new knowledge and skills and reinvest them back into Pakistan.

Popinjay

Popinjay is an ethical business that employs women to produce hand-crafted handbags, which are sold online and the proceeds used to better the lives of its employees. Popinjay, formerly known as Bags for BLISS, is situated in Hafizabad in the Punjab region of Pakistan. The enterprise employs and trains 150 women to deliver handmade embroidery for high-end handbags. Each woman receives a secure wage and through Popinjay is able to connect with the global market to sell their products and ideas. This value creation and promotion of transformational development within a relatively rural male-dominated region in Pakistan demonstrates how the empowerment of women can be achieved. Popinjay's next challenge is to scale up this model throughout Pakistan, driving social change and contributing to the development of a niche industry on a national scale.

Potential Enterprise Mapping Strategy (PEMS)

PEMS an organization that focuses on building and developing grass-roots enterprises in Karachi, with a view to scaling successful models and strategies throughout Pakistan. PEMS started out as a research project investigating what was restricting Karachi-based small-scale enterprises from achieving their goals and delivering social impact. The majority of the barriers identified were around lack of finance, resources, knowledge and expertise. PEMS connected with SEED Ventures, a hub for social entrepreneurship, to provide support, guidance and understanding to these small-scale enterprises. Their next step is to extend the benefits of their research beyond organizations to individual entrepreneurs. As an organization, PEMS is expected to play a critical role in supporting sustainable enterprises in years to come.

Further resources

ThinkChange Pakistan – An online platform for social enterprises and private companies, which promotes awareness about their CSR activities. They partnered with ThinkChange India to showcase news, case studies and jobs in both countries.

Securities and Exchange Commission of Pakistan (SECP) – The financial regulatory body that seeks to develop a modern and efficient corporate sector and a capital market based on sound regulatory principles, in order to encourage investment and foster economic growth and prosperity in Pakistan.

SEED Ventures, Social Economic and Equity Development (SEED) – An organization in Pakistan that invests in start-up enterprises and promotes research around enterprise development. Primarily focused in Karachi, they recently launched a facility that provides office space and mentorship to young entrepreneurs.

References

British Council and YES Network Pakistan (2013). Enterprising Pakistan. Report. London and Islamabad.

Bute, S. (2013). Backgrounder: innovation: the new mantra for science and technology policies in India, Pakistan and China. New Delhi: The Institute for Defence Studies.

CSR WeltWeit (2012). Pakistan: the role of CSR. Gütersloh: CSR WeltWeit.

Invest2innovate (2014). Pakistan entrepreneurship ecosystem report 2014. Islamabad: Invest2innovate.

Pakistan Observer (2014, 7 September). WWF-Pakistan collaborates with daraz.pk for CSR initiative. *Pakistan Observer.*

SECP (Securities and Exchange Commission of Pakistan) (2013). Corporate social responsibility voluntary guidelines 2013. Islamabad: SECP.

Shah, P. & Shubhisham, S. (2012). Social entrepreneurship in Pakistan: unlocking innovation through enterprise incubation. Report for EPG Economic and Strategy Consulting. London.

Social Progress Imperative (2014). Social Progress Index – Pakistan. Washington, DC: Social Progress Imperative.

TDP (Trade Development Authority of Pakistan) (2014). Export statistics and trends. Islamabad: TDAP.

UNDP (United Nations Development Programme) (2013). About Pakistan. New York: UNDP.

15
Papua New Guinea

Tapan Sarker
Discipline Leader, Sustainable Enterprise, Griffith University Business School, Australia
Lorne Butt
Director and Company Secretary, Institute for Sustainable Leadership Ltd and Sustainability Coordinator at TAFE NSW Western Institute, Australia

National context

Papua New Guinea (PNG) consists of a group of around 600 islands, including eastern New Guinea, lying to the north of Australia. PNG is comprised of mainly mountainous and volcanic terrain, with the rest of the country's geography made up of rolling foothills and coastal lowlands. PNG obtained its independence from Australia in 1975. Although PNG is now a constitutional parliamentary democracy, political coalitions are unstable and corruption is prevalent throughout the government sector.

PNG's population of around 6.5 million comprises over 800 known spoken languages and several thousand separate (typically small) communities. PNG is also rich in natural resources, and increasingly focused on economic diversification and sustainable industry. About 85% of the total population live in rural areas, practising small-scale agriculture (Trogolo, 2008).

Key industries include extractives (mainly gold, gas, oil and copper), forestry, fishing (primarily tuna), palm oil, coffee, cocoa, coconut oil, tea, coffee, spices, sugar, sweet potatoes, vanilla, cocoa and rubber. Commodity exports reached $5.6 billion in 2012, comprising mainly oil, gold, copper ore, timber, palm oil, coffee, cocoa and shellfish/prawns. Australia remains PNG's primary import/export partner. However, approximately 40% of the population lives in poverty on less than US$1.00 a day (Trogolo, 2008).

Priority issues

PNG's GDP growth (5.4% in real terms in 2013) and export earnings are heavily dependent on mining. Mining disasters have resulted in significant damage to PNG's environment and resulted in thousands of farmers losing their livelihoods. Discharge of mining waste from the Ok Tedi Mine resulted in damage to over 1,500 km^2 of the Ok Tedi and Fly river catchment areas, and is estimated to have affected the lives of some 50,000 villagers (Marychurch and Stoianoff, 2006).

Other examples where mining operations have caused severe environmental and social disruption include the Ramu nickel mine near Madang, the Lihir gold mine in the New Ireland province, the Panguna copper mine on Bougainville Island, the Tolukuma gold mine north of Port Moresby, and gold mines at Porgera, Misima and Kainantu. While some of these mines, such as Panguna, are not currently operational, the environmental and social impacts of unsustainable extraction and poor waste management practices are likely to continue for generations.

PNG remains an unstable country plagued by poverty, unemployment and violence, with low levels of literacy (only 60% of people over 15 years of age can read and write), poor infrastructure and development, high levels of maternal and infant mortality, and the highest incidence of HIV/Aids in the Pacific region. Approximately 40% of the population is under 15 years of age, and human trafficking for the purposes of sexual slavery and forced labour is endemic.

Unregulated deforestation, pollution of waterways and other associated impacts caused by mining and logging are the main environmental concerns (Trogolo, 2008). However, further agriculture-based development is hampered by only 30% of PNG's landmass being suited to crops, and only 2% overall being suited to permanent farming practices (Trogolo, 2008).

PNG's system of land tenure is a challenge for industry and infrastructure development. While the indigenous people have legal basis to inalienable tenure of traditional lands, there is confusion around issues such as communal ownership by clans, individual ownership of land parcels that may not be further divided, and granting of large-scale agricultural development leases by the government. Freehold title is minimal, with most alienated land held under private lease or government ownership. Economic, social and environmental development and management is affected by this lack of clarity around land ownership due to ongoing disputes around ownership, issues of customary land rights and maintenance of cultural, economic and social associations with land (James *et al.*, 2012).

Trends

Fair Trade certification is gaining the attention of PNG producers as a key promotional strategy for export markets. Hence we see attention given to forming cooperatives, developing business skills and designing accompanying social programmes to support local communities, especially for crops such as cocoa, honey and various spices. Besides social responsibility, the prohibitive cost of purchasing and transporting synthetic agricultural chemicals means that many crops grown in PNG are naturally free from chemicals and pollutants, and therefore meet organic certification standards.

Farmer groups are also examining ways of diversifying crops in order to support sustainable agriculture and decrease dependence on single products. These groups have demonstrated an efficient approach to production with the support of microfinance incentives and obtaining local community support. Further improvements to productivity of up to 60% are anticipated by improvements to agricultural, marketing and selling practices, and processing facilities. This will support production of high-quality outputs and increase prices – despite ongoing challenges related to investment and price fluctuations.

Another trend is community-based eco-tourism operations – either fully PNG-owned and -operated, or operating in conjunction with partner organizations based in Australia and elsewhere – which are growing in PNG, with the Kokoda Track being perhaps PNG's most famous tourist destination.

Efforts to support sustainable enterprise in other industries such as forestry have met with less success in recent years, with smallholdings unable to compete with large companies that use timber concessions granted by the government and exploit cheap labour to log large areas unsustainably. The short-term benefit is cheap prices, but the long-term effects are economic, social, and more importantly environmental damage to the local communities left without sustainable resources to support them once the large companies move elsewhere.

Government policies

The PNG government is working to establish frameworks and support services to improve economic and social development through the expansion of mining, agricultural, forestry and fishery exports, but also through the development of financial products that support small and medium enterprise and new market entrants. Key examples from the PNG Medium Term Development Plan 2011–15 include the promotion of cooperative societies in rural areas as a mechanism for developing agricultural and fisheries enterprises; establishment of microfinance banking agencies; furthering opportunities for eco-tourism and cottage industries; and delivery of training programmes in establishing and running a business.

Sustainable trade and investment, improved natural resource and environmental management, protection of cultural identity and traditional knowledge, and improved governance relating to transparency, accountability, equity and efficiency in the management of resources are central features of various trade agreements and instruments of economic cooperation between PNG and other countries in the Pacific region, including Fiji, and between PNG and organizations such as the United Nations and the European Union.

Case studies

AGOGA Plantation Pty Ltd

AGOGA is a cooperative of coffee producers in PNG, which was founded in 1981 and became the first Fair Trade-certified organization in PNG in 1997. Each cooperative member owns a family plot, and shares a single common 100-hectare plot with the broader cooperative group. Both production and processing are located in PNG's Easter Highlands region, with processing facilities at AGOGA's factory in the village of Tanaranofi, Kainantu. The latest figures indicate that the cooperative benefits over 2,300 family members, with interest from neighbouring farmers to join the organization.

AGOGA exports to the USA and Europe. Since its creation, AGOGA has been able to produce a high-quality coffee product and take advantage of the Fair Trade premium to purchase a wet mill, water tank and depulping machines to further improve the quality of their product. Other projects supporting local health, education and infrastructure initiatives including the provision of college scholarships to young adults in the community, funding the construction of a new elementary school, creating a mobile clinic to service the region, improving road access, and commencing the installation of basic electricity and water services in members' homes.

Cloudy Bay Sustainable Forestry Ltd

Cloudy Bay Sustainable Forestry is a subsidiary of the PNG Sustainable Development Program Ltd and the first timber company in PNG, producing timber and processed wood products such as decking for the local market. Founded during the 1970s as the Northern District Sawmilling and Timber Co. Ltd, the company changed its name to Cloudy Bay Sustainable Forestry in 2007. Several species are managed through the forestry operations – including rosewood, New Guinea walnut and white tulip oak – uses for which range from commercial construction to domestic fit out. Forests are managed on a 35-year cycle.

Cloudy Bay does not use arsenic or chromium in its timber preservation processes, instead using a water-based pressure treatment that includes copper that is registered with the Australian Pesticides and Veterinary Medicines Authority. In addition to harvesting, processing and replanting activity, the company also operates joinery and building divisions that manufacture prefabricated homes and offices, as well as furniture. Cloud Bay also supports various infrastructure and socioeconomic development projects, including schools, health centres, sports facilities, roads, and conservation of sacred and cultural sites. The company achieved Forest Stewardship Council certification in 2013 for responsible forest management.

Cocoa PNG Project

Through the Cocoa PNG Project, Business for Millennium Development (B4MD, 2013) – an independent, Australian-based not-for-profit organization – and Kraft Foods Australia are supporting cocoa farmers in PNG to enhance productivity and gain access to better health and education opportunities in the provinces of Morobe and Madang. Key initiatives relate to training in business skills development, stabilization of prices through production of high-quality cocoa, wider access to inputs such as tools and seed stock, enhanced marketing and implementation of accompanying social programmes such as better resourcing of schools.

Kraft Foods is the world's largest chocolate company. In November 2012, it initiated a major investment project ($400 million over the next ten years) to support expansion of cocoa production by farming communities. The project is expected to support 200,000 farmers directly and 1,000,000 people in the wider communities themselves. As of March 2013, Kraft Foods Australia had partnered with B4MD to develop a business plan that incorporates the initiatives promoted by B4MD in relation to training, price stabilization, marketing, equipment and social programmes.

New Britain Palm Oil Ltd (NBPOL)

NBPOL (2012) is PNG's largest palm oil plantation and milling operator. The company is focused on ensuring its products are sustainably produced and traceable across the supply chain, ensuring that its customers can be confident of the integrity of what they purchase. The company is one of PNG's largest employers (approximately 25,000 employees in 2011) and operates palm oil estates in the Solomon Islands, West New Britain and PNG. NBPOL operates over 77,000 ha of plantations, 12 oil mills, two refineries (one in PNG and the other in Liverpool in the UK), sugar plantations, a 20,000-head beef cattle operation, and a seed production and plant breeding facility. The company exports primarily to the UK, Europe and Australia.

Sustainable management is central to NBPOL's business strategy. A key focus has been the management of a segregated supply chain, and all NBPOL plantations and associated smallholders have been certified by the Roundtable on Sustainable Palm Oil (RSPO). The smallholders are a vital part of the certification process as they directly manage the plantations. In addition, four of NBPOL's 11 crude palm oil mills, and its palm kernel mill, have achieved RSPO certification.

The Higaturu site is a case in point. Acquired in 2010 along with the Poliamba and Milne Bay sites in PNG, Higaturu comprises 8,533 ha of palm, three mills, and 5,708 smallholder blocks producing the largest proportion (44.2%) of NBPOL's fresh fruit bunches for processing. In 2011, 86,788 tonnes of crude palm oil was produced.

RSPO certification assessment of Higaturu commenced in 2012. This followed several years of work to address poor management practices that had resulted in low yields (in some cases, less than 2 tonnes per hectare). NBPOL worked with the local communities to provide credit, training, support and supervision in agricultural management practices; undertook extensive replanting; and created employment opportunities for young people. In one trial area, increases in yields of 120% have been recorded – in 2011; average production of this trial area reached 14 tonnes per hectare. Crime and vandalism have also been reduced.

Further resources

Australian Centre for International Agricultural Research (ACIAR) – ACIAR's research supports projects to increase productivity and improve access to markets for smallholders.

PNG Microfinance Ltd – PNG's first microfinance institution, established in 2004 and providing financial services to the small–medium enterprise sector in PNG.

Roundtable on Sustainable Palm Oil – The RSPO works with the commercial and not-for-profit sectors, governments and producers to support the production and use of sustainable palm oil.

World Bank – Provides loan funding to support projects focused on infrastructure, mining, agriculture and social development programmes focused on PNG's youth.

References

B4MD (Business for Millennium Development) (2013). Field report: cocoa, PNG – March 2013. Melbourne: B4MD.

James, P., Nadarajah, Y., Haive, K. & Stead, V. (2012). *Sustainable communities, sustainable development: other paths for Papua New Guinea*. Honolulu: University of Hawaii Press.

Marychurch, J.M. & Stoianoff, N.P. (2006). Blurring the lines of environmental responsibility: how corporate and public governance was circumvented in the Ok Tedi Mining Limited disaster. 61st Annual ALTA Conference – Legal Knowledge: Learning, Communicating and Doing Lindfield, Australia: Australian Law Teachers Association (ALTA) Secretariat.

NBPOL (New Britain Palm Oil Limited) (2012). Sustainability Report 2010–2011. London: New Britain Palm Oil Limited.

Trogolo, M.J. (2008). Fairtrade development in Papua New Guinea: linking producers in Asia Pacific with traders in Australia and New Zealand. Fair Trade Association of Australia and New Zealand.

16
Philippines

Markus Dietrich
Director, Asian Social Enterprise Incubator (ASEI), The Philippines
Verrome Hutchinson
Programme Manager, Asian Social Enterprise Incubator (ASEI), The Philippines

National context

The Philippines is located in South-East Asia and is a large archipelago made up of over 7,000 islands, with an area of 300,000 km^2 which is categorized into three island groups: Luzon, Visayas and Mindanao. It has a market-based economy with a GDP of $250 billion (2012) and a GDP per capita of $2,500.

The Philippines is a presidential republic with the current president, Benigno Aquino III, enjoying high popularity as a result of his good governance and reform agenda. The last five years have seen the Philippines experience strong economic growth, making it one of the fastest growing countries in the region and the 28th largest economy in the world.

With a population of over 100 million, growing at 1.7% annually, the Philippines is the 12th most populous country in the world and the second most populous in the ASEAN-6 region.

Priority issues

Until recently, economic growth in the Philippines lagged behind its South-East Asian neighbours. However, from 2011 to 2013 the country experienced strong GDP growth, with rates of 3.7%, 6.8% and 7.2% respectively. Despite this progress, the Philippines continue to experience persistent high poverty, unemployment and a lack of access to basic services for the low-income population.

The economy, which is mainly consumption driven and supported by remittances from overseas foreign workers – who sent back over $22 billion (8.5% of GDP) in 2013 – is not creating a sufficient number of jobs. Instead, it has the highest unemployment rate in the ASEAN region with 7.5% or 2.9 million Filipinos unemployed as of January 2014.

The World Bank (2013) Ease of Doing Business ranks the country at 108 out of 189. These difficulties, as well as the investment policy that does not allow for full foreign ownership, has been attributed to the low flow of Foreign Direct Investment (FDI), with the country receiving only $2.79 billion in net FDI out of an approximate total of $109 billion that flowed into the ASEAN region in 2012.

The poverty rate stays persistently around 25%, equivalent to 4.2 million poor families in 2012, with a concentration in the rural areas. The majority of the population is categorized as low income, earning between $1.25 and $3 a day from working in the agricultural and informal sector. It is estimated that informal workers make up over 42% of the total working population.

While significant progress has been made in achieving the UN Millennium Development Goals (MDGs), the Philippines still lags behind on a number of health indicators, the achievement of universal primary education and combating HIV/Aids. In addition, there are still 16 million people who do not have access to clean drinking water and electricity and approximately 3 million who live in informal settlements in Metro Manila alone.

While naturally resource-rich, the Philippines is also the third most disaster-prone country in the world and susceptible to adverse weather such as typhoons, earthquakes and volcanic eruptions, which have a significant impact on the country's economic performance. Usually, the country's low-income populations are worst affected, as evidenced by typhoon Haiyan in 2013.

Trends

In the Philippines, sustainable enterprises are classified in two categories: social enterprises denoting start-up organizations with social impact, and inclusive businesses (IB) defined as medium to large companies creating social impact at scale and with high financial returns (Red Mantra Group, 2013). Thus far, the conversation on IB and social enterprises has been largely driven by multilateral organizations such as the Asian Development Bank (ADB), with business associations joining in and academic institutions conducting research and teaching on social entrepreneurship (Asian Development Bank, 2011).

The Asian Social Enterprise Incubator (ASEI) conducted a market scoping study on inclusive business in 2012 for the ADB (Asian Social Enterprise Incubator, 2013). It was found at the time that the IB space was "nascent", with only a small number of companies, financial institutions and donors active in the sector. However, ASEI has seen the space developing rapidly and in 2014 it can be classified as an "emerging" sector.

The Ateneo de Manila University (2012) carried out a study on the state of social enterprises in the Philippines. The study found that over 30,000 organizations could potentially be classified as social enterprises with the vast majority being cooperatives and microfinance institutions. Apart from those, it was found that social enterprise is a very young sector experiencing challenges in scaling up, accessing funding and a lack of a systematic organization to aid their development.

Reports conducted for the League of Corporate Foundations found that corporate foundations are moving away from traditional approaches and have begun to develop inclusive business models such as integrating low-income people into the value chains of the company or Creating Shared Value (CSV) models (Rimando, 2012). Therefore the focus for sustainable enterprises is on integrating inclusive business models into mainstream businesses and upscaling the activities of social enterprises.

Government policies

While the government has assigned a high importance to inclusive growth, it has not developed an explicit strategy for mainstreaming inclusive business into the development agenda beyond the private sector's role in public–private partnerships, especially as it pertains to infrastructure laid down in the Philippines Development Plan 2011–16.

There are, however, a number of government agencies, such as the Board of Investments, currently conducting pilot programmes, which could result in more institutional support for IB and creating an enabling environment.

In April 2012, House Bill #6085, the Magna Carta for Social Enterprises was submitted to congress, although this law has not been enacted into law. The main objective of this bill is to create an enabling environment for social enterprises by introducing incentives such as preferential access to government procurement and support services such as marketing and capital development.

Case studies

Generika Drugstore

Generika Drugstore is a chain of pharmacies all across the Philippines, which provides low-cost medicine and diagnostic health education and services to the low-income population. They provide consumer education on medicine use and application and free basic check-ups, as well as providing millions of customers with access to affordable and safe medicine. Generika has developed a nationwide branch network through partnerships with selected suppliers. Franchising is seen as the main engine of growth for the business and to date, they have opened 360 stores, of which 25 are company owned.

Jollibee Foods Corporation (JFC)

Jollibee Foods Corporation (JFC) is a large Philippine multinational fast food chain of restaurants. In 2007, the Jollibee board made a strategic decision to move beyond their Corporate Social Responsibility (CSR) approach to adopt the Creating Shared Value (CSV) model. The Farmer Entrepreneurship Program (FEP) links smallholder farmers to the Jollibee supply chain through the provision of red bulb onions, thus resulting in increased incomes and livelihoods. Included in the programme is also intensive entrepreneurship training and access to credit through the help of partner finance institutions.

Since changing their focus from philanthropy to CSV, Jollibee has directly engaged with 700 farmers and plans to expand this to 8,000 in 2015, while also sourcing other types of produce from farmers. Since starting the FEP, JFC has partnered with over 40 companies and local institutions to replicate its success and developed over 900 farmers, with 12 companies currently sourcing directly from farmers for their vegetable needs.

Kennemer Foods International Inc (KFI)

Kennemer Foods International Inc (KFI) is a producer and marketer of food and agricultural products and is focused on growing and trading high-quality fermented cacao beans. KFI was founded in 2010 initially to source cacao beans for international customers. However, it became apparent that the Philippines did not have an adequate supply of cacao beans and the industry was dormant. As a result, KFI expanded its business model to include local production by setting up a contract-growing programme in rural areas and extending company-owned nurseries.

To date, KFI has engaged with 3,700 "bottom of the pyramid" farmers on a contract-farming basis (70% were earning less than $2 a day and the remaining 30% less than $3 a day). KFI is in the process of upscaling their activities, which they estimate will result in the creation of over 30,000 jobs and planting of over 30 million trees.

Manila Water

Manila Water was privatized at a time when only 58% of the population had access to serviced water and the rest had to rely on obtaining water from public faucets, buying it from vendors at high prices or illegally acquiring it from nearby pipes. Manila Water created its inclusive business model, Tubig Para Sa Barangay (TPSB), to solve this problem of access. To date, not only is the company one of the few profitable utilities companies in the world with a net income of $130 million, but it has also reached over 1.6 million people and provided access to clean and safe water. The Department of Health reported a 300% reduction in water-borne diseases from 1997 to 2007 and it estimated that since inception, the business model has generated over $0.5 million of income from new jobs.

Phinma Property Holdings Corporation

Phinma Property Holdings Corporation is focused on the development of low-cost housing. Phinma entered into the first successful public–private partnership with Quezon City, a local government authority, to develop

Bistekville II, the first private-sector-led inner-city relocation project in the country. Bistekville II consists of 705 row houses and is targeted at the top end of the "base of the pyramid" market, or those earning the equivalent of US$405 per month.

It is estimated that at least 500,000 families in Manila live in informal settlements and the replacement value of informal to formal housing is estimated to be over $600 million. The successful completion of this pilot will be a model for replication by other housing developers to supply the much-needed housing demand in the country.

Further resources

League of Corporate Foundations – LCF is a network of over 80 foundations that promote and enhance the strategic practice of CSR among its members. One of its main agendas is the promotion of inclusive growth through targeted strategies such as linking small-scale entrepreneurs to big business as a market outlet.

Makati Business Club – MBC is a business association with the main aim of promoting the role of the private sector in the country's development efforts, including the planning and implementation of relevant policies, investment promotion and corporate citizenship initiatives.

Management Association of the Philippines – MAP is an organization consisting of business executives from the largest local and multinational companies in the Philippines. One of their main advocacies is the promotion of inclusive growth by encouraging reforms and economic policies that are conducive for the promotion of investments and the creation of jobs.

Philippine Business for the Environment – PBE is the Philippines representative for the World Business Council for Sustainable Development (WBCSD) and is responsible for the implementation of environmental programmes in the Philippines. It has recently developed an initiative for sustainable forestry for its members.

Philippine Business for Social Progress – PBSP is a foundation comprised of over 200 businesses and whose aim is to contribute to poverty reduction. It has created the Inclusive Business Imperative, which is a nationwide campaign to promote IB as a core business activity through capacity building of relevant stakeholders, impact assessments and knowledge sharing among others.

References

Asian Development Bank (2011). Impact investors in Asia: characteristics and preferences for investing in social enterprises in Asia and the Pacific. Manila: ADB.

Asian Social Enterprise Incubator (2013). Inclusive business study – Philippines. Report for the Asian Development Bank. Manila: ASEI.

Ateneo de Manila University (2012). The state of social enterprises in the Philippines. Unpublished report.

Red Mantra Group (2013). Working together in pursuit of inclusive business: sharing the Latin American and Caribbean experience with Asia and the Pacific. Report for the Asian Development Bank and the Inter-American Development Bank.

Rimando, L. (2012). How CSR is evolving in the Philippines. *Rappler*, 6 April 2012.

World Bank (2013). Doing Business 2014. Washington, DC.

17
Singapore

Thomas Thomas
Chief Executive Officer, ASEAN CSR Network, Singapore

National context

In the 1960s, following Singapore's independence, the economy was constrained by a number of limiting factors: few natural resources, little local capital, small size of educated population and labour unrest. The government needed to create a conducive environment for businesses to invest, create quality jobs and raise people's living standards and quality of life. Tripartism was thus established as a consultative decision-making framework in which government, labour and business could collectively mobilize human, financial and natural resources equitably and efficiently to promote sustainable enterprises and address the challenges of industrialization.

Another important milestone in promoting sustainable enterprises was the formation of the National Tripartite Initiative on Corporate Social Responsibility in May 2004 (Wong, 2011). It was launched to promote sustainable development for businesses and stakeholders. It had representatives from the government, unions and the business sector, including the National Trades Union Congress and the Singapore National Employers Federation. It went on to found a national CSR society in January 2005, called the Singapore Compact for Corporate Social Responsibility. Singapore Compact is also the focal point and network body for the United

Nations Global Compact, the Global Reporting Initiative and a founder member of the ASEAN CSR Network (ACN) – a regional network of CSR networks.

The concept of sustainable enterprises has continued to grow in importance and significance (Wong, 2011). Sustainable enterprises are a principal source of growth, wealth creation, employment and decent work. The promotion of sustainable enterprise is, therefore, a major tool for achieving sustainable development and innovation that improve standards of living and social, environmental conditions over time (ILO, 2007). In Singapore these enterprises are known as socially responsible enterprises. Sustainability and sustainable enterprises are outcomes of social responsibility.

Priority issues

In the last decade, the Singaporean economy has fared well, averaging 5% annual growth despite many difficult challenges. Productivity growth over the same period averaged about 1% per annum. Productivity gains declined in recent years due to heavier reliance on labour inputs, especially inputs of foreign workers. Productivity-driven growth will require major new investments in the skills, expertise and innovative capabilities of Singaporeans and businesses within every sector of the economy over the next decade.

The priorities in the next phase of economic restructuring will include a focus on SME upgrading, preparing Singaporeans for the jobs of the future and for management practices to change to meet the new challenges. CSR needs to be seen as essential to economic success as well as social justice (Balakrishnan's 2008 speech, in Tan, 2011).

Singapore fulfils most of its resource needs through imports. It therefore has to improve its efficiency in using resources such as energy, water and land. Sustainable Singapore Blueprint 2009 identified major targets to meet these goals. A cleaner, greener environment has improved the quality of life of Singaporeans, and made it more attractive to investors and visitors. However, it suffers from cross-boundary haze from neighbouring countries. In June 2013, air pollution soared to a record 401 on the Pollutant Standards Index. The incident highlights the vulnerability of Singapore towards the regional and global problem of deforestation and climate change. Singapore needs to make further efforts to improve its air quality, conserve natural biodiversity and make the city cleaner and greener.

Trends

A CSR survey conducted in 2008 by the Ministry of Trade and Industry (MTI) (2008) for Singapore Compact on 507 Singapore-based companies showed a relatively low level of understanding and awareness of CSR in Singapore. It was understood as paying back to society, through philanthropy and volunteerism; 60% agreed that profitability should be balanced by their contributions to the wider public good, while 40% still saw CSR as merely compliance (Tan, 2011).

In June 2011, the Singapore Exchange (SGX) introduced a Sustainability Reporting Guide to encourage listed companies to extend their reporting beyond financial governance to sustainability aspects. Singapore Compact conducted research in 2011 and 2014 to assess the state of voluntary sustainability reporting among companies listed on the SGX Main Board at the end of 2010 and 2013 respectively.

The 2011 research found out that only 79 companies, or about 14%, have engaged in sustainability reporting activities. This was a 25% increase from 64 companies in 2009. Only ten companies used the GRI framework. The reports also showed that most companies still consider CSR as simply giving back to the community as opposed to being responsible for the business' impact on society and creating sustainable practices for long-term development (Thomas and Chin, 2011).

The 2014 study found out that there were 160 companies, or 30%, communicating their sustainability efforts. This represents a twofold increase from 79 companies in 2011. The number of companies adopting the GRI framework to produce their sustainability reports also rose from ten in 2011 to 19 companies in 2013.

Government policies

Over the last 50 years, the Singaporean government has succeeded in putting in place a comprehensive set of regulations that have established high standards of responsible and sustainable business practices (Sim,

2013). These were under a framework of norms and practices to reinforce responsible business conduct.

The Code of Corporate Governance was first implemented in 2001, revised in 2005 and came under the purview of the Monetary Authority of Singapore (MAS) and Singapore Exchange (SGX) with effect from September 2007. Compliance with the Code is not mandatory but listed companies are required to disclose their corporate governance practices and give explanations for deviations from the Code in their annual reports. The revision of the Code in May 2012 states that the role of the Board is to "consider sustainability issues, e.g. environmental and social factors, as part of its strategic formulation".

An Inter-Ministerial Committee for Sustainable Development (IMCSD) was set up in 2008 to formulate a clear national framework and strategy for sustainable development in Singapore in the context of emerging domestic and global changes. It also spearheads the Sustainable Singapore Blueprint of strategies and initiatives to achieve both economic growth and a good living environment.

A variety of environmental protection and management regulations set standards on various issues such as emission control, ozone-depleting substances, energy conservation, public cleansing, toxic industrial waste and quality of piped drinking water. Employment and industrial relations practices are covered by legislation and tripartite guidelines such as the Industrial Relations Act, Employment Act, Central Provident Fund Act, Retirement and Re-employment Act.

Case studies

Adrenalin Events and Education

Established in 2008, Adrenalin group is a social enterprise events agency with the purpose of organizing "events with heart". Setting the target that 30% of their events will have an element of giving back, Adrenalin has helped raise S$1.2 million (US$960,000) for various causes and mobilized 10,000 volunteer hours for the community. Furthermore, it has extended its social mission to employing and training physically challenged, deaf and youth at risk as part of its team. Environmental protection is also a priority for Adrenalin, through environmentally friendly initiatives such as printing name cards on recycled paper and choosing greener suppliers.

Keppel Land Limited

Keppel Land is the property arm of Keppel Corporation, one of Singapore's largest conglomerates established in 1968, with interests in offshore and marine infrastructure and property. The environment and workplace safety form the main pillars of Keppel Land's sustainability programme, in which the company constantly looks for innovative green technology, eco-friendly and energy-saving features and processes, as well as safety measures to become a "zero harm" workplace. Keppel Land's annual sustainability report, launched in 2008, includes the company's key goals and achievements.

Origin Exterminators Pte Ltd

Origin Exterminators is a local SME specializing in tropical pest control. Since its inception in 1991, the company has defined itself as a responsible steward of the environment. Instead of traditional methods of pest control which release large volumes of insecticides and other chemicals into the environment, Origin developed new methods to realize its goal of providing environmentally friendly and proactive pest control solutions. Furthermore, the company has moved beyond its pest control business to provide environmental consultancy services to other pest control companies in order to promote sustainability across the industry. Health protection and safety for employees is also a priority of Origin, demonstrated by a comprehensive set of safety modules integrated in the company's training programmes. Sound business practices that promote sustainable development have won Origin support from the more discerning customers, at home and in the region. The company's sustainability reports produced annually since 2005–2006 provide good insight into its CSR commitment and practices.

NTUC FairPrice Co-operative Ltd

NTUC FairPrice was established in 1973 as a social enterprise with a social mission to moderate the cost of living for its members and for the Singapore community. To realize its vision to be Singapore's leading world-class retailer with a heart, FairPrice defines its business model as CSR-driven with four key priorities: Responsible Retailing, Community Care, Sustainable Environment and Wonderful Workplace. FairPrice's success can be demonstrated by not only its increased year-on-year revenues and 52% dominant market share, but also by the success and public recognition of its various CSR programmes, such as price moderation, product safety and safe food handling, good human resource practices, education scholarships, creative environmental initiatives and other strategic initiatives. The FairPrice Online CSR Report, launched in 2011, is an ongoing sustainability report that details the company's CSR initiatives and practices.

Siloso Beach Resort

Siloso Beach Resort is an eco-hotel opened in 2006. At the heart of the hotel's business and its management decisions is sustainability and CSR. Siloso is designed and operated in an innovative and environmentally friendly way which helps save energy, maintain biodiversity and protect ecosystems, while providing a high-quality experience for its guests. Training on work practices and ethical principles, work–life balance, and wellness programmes are provided and promoted for employees of Siloso, of whom many are from various disadvantaged groups. The hotel is also active in sharing information on sustainability through various projects, such as the Biodiversity Portal of Singapore, or educational programmes and eco-tours on sustainability practices. Through these initiatives, Siloso is able to influence its guests and other stakeholders from other countries to embrace the sustainability cause in their own countries.

Further resources

Consumers Association of Singapore – CASE is committed towards protecting consumers' interests through information and education, and promoting an environment of fair and ethical trade practices.

National Trades Union Congress – NTUC is a national federation of trade unions in Singapore. It helps working people to earn a better living and live a better life.

Singapore Business Federation – SBF is the apex business chamber championing the interests of the Singapore business community. SBF has a Sustainable Development Group to promote sustainable practices.

Singapore Compact for CSR – The national society raising awareness and building the capacity of organizations under a multi-stakeholder framework in responsible and sustainable business conduct (www.csrsingapore. org).

Singapore Environment Council – SEC's main objectives include promoting greater public awareness of and concern for the living and natural environment, and encouraging the public to be more environmentally conscious and developing a greater sense of environmental responsibility.

References

ILO (2007). Conclusions concerning the promotion of sustainable enterprises, International Labour Conference. Geneva: ILO.

Ministry of Trade and Industry (2008). National CSR survey. Singapore: Singapore Compact for CSR.

Sim, J. (ed.) (2013). *Many journeys, common destination.* Singapore: Singapore Institute of Management.

Tan, E.K.B. (2011). The state of play of CSR in Singapore. Singapore: Lien Centre for Social Innovation.

Thomas, T., & Chin, H. (2011). Sustainability reporting in Singapore: non-financial reporting among mainboard listed companies in Singapore – a view of the sustainability reporting landscape in 2010–2011. Singapore Compact for CSR.

Wong, E. (ed.) (2011). *Socially responsible and sustainable: company perspective and experiences.* Singapore: Straits Times Press.

18
South Korea

Angela Joo-Hyun Kang
Founder and Executive President, Global Competitiveness Empowerment Forum (GCEF),
South Korea

National context

South Korea, officially the Republic of Korea, is located in the southern half of the Korean Peninsula in East Asia with a population of 51 million. It was established by the founding father, Dangun, as Go-Joseon in 2,333 BC. The Shilla Dynasty emerged as a unified country on the peninsula in 668 and the nation flourished in the following centuries, except for the Japanese colonization period (1910–45). It was divided into South and North Korea in the aftermath of the Korean War (1950–53).

From all the hardships, South Korea pulled off what is known as "the Miracle on the Han River" with a series of five-year economic development plans crafted and implemented by the government's leadership starting from 1962. With successful industrialization and democratization, the country transformed itself from an aid recipient in the 1960s to a donor and G20 member. It's also the 15th largest world economic power with $23,837 GDP per capita in 2013.

South Korea's business community has been a powerful force in the country's push for economic development. The key growth engines are exports, which contribute 56% of GDP, and large conglomerates, known as Chaebol, with 84% of sales relative to GDP made by the top ten Chaebol groups in 2012. South Korea's trade volume reached $1 trillion in 2011 as the seventh largest exporter and it aims to achieve $2 trillion by 2020.

The founding philosophy of South Korea is Hong-Ik-In-Gan (弘益人間, benefiting all humankind widely), with a long tradition of respecting stakeholder interests, influenced by Buddhism, Confucianism, Christianity and Chondogyo (Kang and Lee, 2010). From 2013, the Park Geun-hye administration has emphasized "creative economy". This national agenda has encouraged South Korean corporations to adopt "creating shared value" (CSV) and sustainability, which are closely related with one of the Confucianism values, Zhong-Yong (中庸, doctrine of the mean) to pursue the ideal of moderation by avoiding excesses and deficiencies (Kang and Lee, 2010).

Priority issues

South Korea's Gini's Coefficient was 0.302 in 2013, an average level among OECD member countries, but Korean people believe there is more inequality than the official figure suggests. According to the research by the Economic Reform Research Institute, the median value of Gross National Income (GNI) is 40% less than the GNI per capita, while the top 1% income value is 90% higher. Overall and youth unemployment rates were 4.5% and 10.9%, respectively, in February 2014 – the highest figures during the past six years. The Korean public is calling for more economic democratization and stimulus policies simultaneously.

Income disparity worsens social and ideological conflicts between "haves" and "have-nots" and between conservatives and liberals. According to the Samsung Economic Research Institute's 2013 Social Conflict Index, South Korea ranked second after Turkey among OECD countries. The cost resulting from social conflicts is measured at 72% of the 2014 government budget. Calls for public and business policies to mitigate social polarization are on the rise.

South Korean corporations have actively responded to domestic and international environmental regulations by considering them as both risks and opportunities. The 2013 Carbon Disclosure Project surveyed the top 250 companies in South Korea and found that 90% have climate change risk management governance. Hence, many companies push for developing low-carbon and high-efficiency technologies and strengthening compliance, while paying attention to government policy directions, including the 37% target for greenhouse gas reduction by 2030, as compared with business as usual.

Trends

To resolve polarization between Chaebols and small and medium enterprises (SMEs), the National Commission for Corporate Partnership evaluates win–win growth and benefit-sharing efforts of the top 100 Chaebols, culminating in an annual Win–Win Index and a prescription of which business items are to be avoided by Chaebols.

The Ministry of Employment and Labor and its affiliated Korea Social Enterprise Promotion Agency have provided a definition of social enterprise, authorized their certification and provided financial and tax supports beginning from 2007. As of 2013, 950 certified social enterprises created 13,108 jobs for the disadvantaged, with 27% average annual growth (Korea Social Enterprise Promotion Agency, 2013). Based on this successful result, the social economy concept was proposed as a strategy for more inclusive growth and resilient community development.

According to the survey of 63 companies listed on the Korea Composite Stock Price Index (KOSPI) by the Korea Social Responsibility Institute and Merry Year Social Company (2014), 71% interpret CSR activities as corporate philanthropy, 51% as social responsibility, 30% as sustainability, 14% as business ethics, 13% social responsibility management, and 11% as creating shared value (CSV). In the survey, it was found that 70% of surveyed companies have an independent CSR team and 80% want to improve their CSR strategy. This means that South Korean companies are in a transition stage from a philanthropic to a strategic approach with broader impacts. The Korean Academy Society Business Administration seized this trend by proposing the CSV Society in 2013.

The above survey found 68% published a CSR or sustainability report, while 82% called for more institutional incentives and 45% pointed out the necessity of public procurement benefits. According to the research by Corporate Governance Service (Ahn, 2013), 98 listed companies have published 338 sustainability reports from 2008 to 2013. It can be said that those companies active in sustainability and responsibility prefer to have regulatory recognition and incentives.

Korea Trade-Investment Promotion Agency (KOTRA), with 122 overseas business centres in 84 countries, has shown support for the global CSR and CSV practices of South Korean corporations since 2012. According to a survey by the Better Future of the Chosunilbo of 50 South Korean public and private enterprises operating in foreign countries, 95% practise global CSR and 67% think that it has positive impacts on their business (Jung *et al.*, 2014).

Government policies

The government policy nurturing sustainable enterprises began with the addition of the ninth clause of the Industrial Development Act (July 2007) by the Ministry of Trade, Industry and Energy. In order to support CSR among SMEs, the eighth clause of the Promotion of Small and Medium Enterprises Act (December 2012) was added by the Small and Medium Business Administration.

A revision of the Financial Investment Services and Capital Market Act was proposed by lawmakers in July 2013 for mandating information disclosure on sustainability and responsibility by listed companies. A revision of the National Pension Act to integrate ESG (environmental, social and governance) considerations into investment decisions, proposed in August 2013, was enacted in January 2015. For socially responsible public procurement, revision of the Government Procurement Act and the Act on Contracts to Which the State is a Party was proposed in December 2014. Also, the Framework Act on Social Value was proposed in June 2014 to prioritize social values in public procurement and governmental development projects.

The Framework Act on Low Carbon, Green Growth (April 2010) was enacted to encourage green technologies and industries. Through its Article 46, Introduction of Cap and Trade System and the Act on the Allocation and Trading of Greenhouse Gas Emission Permits (March 2013), the government introduced a system for trading emissions of greenhouse gas in 2015.

In order to create jobs for the disadvantaged, the Social Enterprise Promotion Act (July 2007) was introduced. For more comprehensive solutions, the Framework Act on Social Economy was proposed in April 2014 to consolidate the fragmented policy programmes run by different ministries.

Case studies

Delight Hearing Aid

In 2009, three university students started their ambitious project to deliver good news to those with hearing impairments who cannot afford to buy expensive hearing aids. Delight Hearing Aid is a social enterprise selling an affordable hearing aid, which they achieved by innovating product design, ensuring mass-market production and discovering new distribution channels via the internet and company-operated stores. Within five years, its sales reached $8 million. It received an award from the Ministry of Trade, Industry and Energy and won the certification of "B Corporation" in 2013, marking the first certified company in north-east Asia.

Hyundai Motor Company

In the automotive industry, sustainability is no longer a new concept. Automotive companies are actively grappling with which technology inno-vations should be supported and the best timing for mass production of eco-friendly cars. Hyundai Motor Company is a global pioneer and front-runner in hydrogen-powered fuel cell vehicles. The Hyundai Tucson Fuel Cell, equipped with next-generation zero-emission vehicle technology and an innovative recharging time that is cut dramatically to three minutes, was launched in Europe, America and South Korea in 2014 (Seo, 2014). It received strong support from government agencies, such as the California Air Resources Board, which is in charge of developing up to 100 hydrogen refuelling stations in the state over the next several years.

Hyundai Motor Company's vision, "A Lifetime Partner Beyond Automobiles", has been inspired by its slogan "New Thinking, New Possibilities". Hyundai's rigorous R&D efforts to create a smart car for everyone, including the physically challenged, and zero-waste endeavours with end-of-life vehicle recycling are based on its commitment to tackle social and environmental challenges.

LG Electronics

LG Electronics (LGE) is widely known as a leader of sustainability and responsibility, which can be traced back to its foundation philosophy, In-Hwa (人和, harmony). The company encourages its employees to live and work based on its action principle of Jeong-Do (正道, going to the right way) management.

Union Social Responsibility is LGE's new paradigm of industrial relations based on the shared commitment of labour and management (Kim *et al.*, 2013). Its global sourcing policy to keep "conflict minerals" out of its global supply chain was showcased in the joint UN Global Compact–PRI publication, "Responsible Business Advancing Peace: Examples from Companies, Investors & Global Compact Local Networks" in 2013.

LGE's special LTE smartphone helps the blind to overcome the digital divide by delivering the sound of characters in a touch-based interface with reinforced TalkBack functionality and providing 7,500 voice books through a Reading Library app. Thanks to LGE's R&D efforts to develop eco-friendly products, 79 of its models acquired the "2012 Energy Star Most Efficient" certificate in 2012, up 600% from the previous year.

POSCO

Listed as "the World's Most Competitive Steelmaker" by World Steel Dynamics for the seventh time in a row (2010–14; twice in 2010 and 2013), POSCO has excelled in integrating sustainability and responsibility into its business. Its renowned innovative technology, FINEX (fine ore reduction process) is a simplified iron-making process, reducing not only cost and time but also coal usage and air pollution (Seo, 2014).

This economically and environmentally creative technology caught the attention of the government of the People's Republic of China. In 2014, a formal joint project contract was co-signed between POSCO and the state-owned Chongqing Iron and Steel Company for technology transfer and building a FINEX integrated steel plant with an annual capacity of 3 million tonnes.

POSCO was ranked 30th in Corporate Knights' 2012 "The Global 100: World Leaders in Clean Capitalism", which lists the world's most sustainable enterprises. POSCO was the only South Korean company in the top half of the list. In 2014, POSCO also incorporated the requirements of the UN's "Protect, Respect and Remedy" Framework for Business and Human Rights into its internal regulations for domestic and global operations, the first South Korean company to do so.

Samsung Electronics

Driven by its belief and commitment for creating shared value (CSV), next-generation products of Samsung Electronics have made positive impacts on society and the Earth.

For African customers, many of whom live in harsh weather conditions, Samsung developed specially designed products that can withstand power outages and voltage fluctuations, such as the Triple Protection TV, Triple Protector Air Conditioner and DuraCool Refrigerator. These high-efficiency products are designed to have no breakdown, while lowering electricity bills. This thoughtful glocalization helped Samsung be ranked No.1 of the most admired brands as well as the most valued brand in the electronics industry in Africa by Brand Leadership Academy collaborating with TNS and Brand Finance.

There are approximately 500,000 data centres around the world, consuming 1.5% of the world's electricity annually and producing annual gas emissions equivalent to 40 million consumer cars. Big data and cloud computing make this situation worse. Samsung Green Memory is designed to increase efficiency and performance as well as lower electricity consumption and costs. If all server systems adopted Samsung Green Memory, the anticipated power saving would be 45 terawatts per year, which is estimated to be worth nearly $3.1 billion. This saving could power the smartphones of 6 billion people for two years, and would have the same carbon-reduction effect of planting 800 million ten-year-old trees.

Further resources

Business Institute for Sustainable Development of Korea Chamber of Commerce and Industry (KCCI-BISD) – As an affiliated organization of the Korean Chamber of Commerce and Industry (KCCI), BISD is committed to pursuing the sustainable development of South Korea through economic growth, preservation of the environment and social development.

Global Compact Network Korea (GCNK) – As a local network of the UN Global Compact in South Korea, GCNK promotes values of human rights, labour, environment and anti-corruption. GCNK has 290 members from government, business, civil society and academia, etc., as of December 2015.

Global Competitiveness Empowerment Forum (GCEF) – Registered under the Ministry of Trade, Industry and Commerce (MOTIE), GCEF promotes CSR, sustainability and business integrity of public, private and social enterprises through research, education, policy analysis and suggestion and multi-stakeholder dialogues.

Global Green Growth Institute (GGGI) – GGGI is an intergovernmental organization headquartered in Seoul, South Korea, to promote low-carbon and sustainable economic growth, known as "green growth", of developing and emerging countries by interdisciplinary and multi-stakeholder approaches.

Institute for Industrial Policy Studies (IPS) – Researches and advises industrial policies for public and private sectors with its 33 research centres working with experts and researchers. Since 2014 the IPS has awarded the 'CSV Porter Prize' to companies in South Korea with excellence in sustainability.

Korea Social Enterprise Promotion Agency (KoSEA) – As an affiliated organization of the Ministry of Employment and Labor, KoSEA fosters and promotes social enterprises by authorizing certification of social enterprises and providing financial, tax, educational and promotional supports.

Korea Social Responsibility Institute (KOSRI) – KOSRI is a private research institute to promote and encourage social responsibility (SR) of corporations, individuals and organizations through research, conferences, SR magazine publishing and awareness-raising activities.

Sustainability Management Center of Korea Standards Association – As an affiliated centre of Korea Standards Association and the ISO 26000 secretariat of South Korea commissioned by Korean Agency for Technology and Standards, Sustainability Management Center provides comprehensive solutions to nurture sustainable enterprises.

Sustainability Services Center of Korea Productivity Center – As an affiliated centre of Korea Productivity Center, Sustainability Services Center provides various solutions to support sustainable enterprises through research, consulting, education and training, etc.

References

Ahn, S.-A. (2013). Analysis of sustainability report publication status by the listed companies of South Korea. *Corporate Governance Service*, Review 68, CSR Status III, 94.

Jung, Y-J., Choi, T-W., Kim, K-H., Moon, S.-H., & Joo, S.-Y. (2014, 14 January). [The Better Future] 95% of South Korean companies in overseas practice global CSR. *The Chosunilbo.*

Kang, A.J.-H. & Lee, S.Y.-S. (2010). South Korea. In W. Visser & N. Tolhurst (Eds.), *World Guide to CSR: A Country-by-Country Analysis of Corporate Sustainability and Responsibility* (pp. 371-377). Sheffield, UK: Greenleaf Publishing.

Kim, Y.-K., Bae, S.-H., & Kwon, S.-W. (2013). *Union social responsibility.* Seoul: Nanam.

Korea Social Enterprise Promotion Agency (2013). *2013 social enterprise directory 950.* Seoul: Korea Social Enterprise Promotion Agency.

Korea Social Responsibility Institute & Merry Year Social Company (2014). *Presentation of 2014 analysis about survey of South Korean companies.* Special session of 2014 CSR International Conference. Seoul, South Korea. 22 May 2014. Seoul: eToday and KOSRI.

Seo, M.-H. (2014, 19 June). Awakened by CSV, corporations making products to benefit the world. *Money Today.*

19
Sri Lanka

M. Rizvi Zaheed
Vice Chairman, CSR Sri Lanka, Sri Lanka

Chandula Abeywickrema
Chairman, CSR Sri Lanka, Sri Lanka

Kaumadee Weeraratne
Head of Operations, CSR Sri Lanka, Sri Lanka

Khadeeja Balkhi
Director of Sustainability, Balkhi Strategy Group, Pakistan

National context

The pearl of the Indian Ocean, Sri Lanka is a 65,610 km^2 tropical island. A 1,600 km coastline skirts the island's diverse topography while a central mountainous region raises elevations to 2,500 m. Since the 200-nautical-mile Exclusive Economic Zone declaration of 1978, Sri Lanka has rights over 517,000 km^2 of the ocean – almost eight times the country's land area.

The island has a population of 21 million with a strong democratic tradition and per capita income of $3,280 with a target of $7,000 by 2020. A 90% literacy rate, investments in infrastructure and a high UN Human Development Index score of 0.715 (against the global average of 0.694) have helped achieve average GDP growth rates of 7% over the past five years (Central Bank of Sri Lanka, 2013).

Policy frameworks supporting private local and foreign investment have boosted economic activity and value creation. Agriculture accounts for 11% of GDP, manufacturing 31% and services 58%. However, much of the growth is skewed towards the western province, which holds 29% of the national population, yet accounts for 42% of the per capita income. As a result, measures are being put in place to promote inclusive growth throughout the nation (Central Bank of Sri Lanka, 2013).

Sri Lanka has a strong tradition of philanthropy – with defensive, charitable or promotional approaches to CSR generally evident among businesses. Though many corporations listed on the Colombo Stock Exchange and beyond speak of sustainability initiatives and produce GRI sustainability reports, such initiatives are often not firmly integrated into corporate strategy.

This is starting to change, as the past five years have seen a growing trend, arising from increasing awareness of social and environmental issues, of sustainable practices and enterprises focusing on transformational impacts.

Priority issues

Youth empowerment and social entrepreneurship are significant priorities for Sri Lanka, which has faced two major youth uprisings: in the early 1970s and again in the late 1980s. Unrest among university communities continues today with the underlying causes not sufficiently addressed. More work is required to provide opportunities for participation and realization of youth aspirations.

Despite the high literacy rates, Sri Lanka's education system needs to be revamped, to gear policies and the curriculum towards greater employability and relevance to the country's skills requirements and human resource needs.

Most conglomerates in Sri Lanka are launching internal "health and welfare" programmes for employees and families. These include awareness building, clinics, annual check-ups and insurance schemes. Even so, according to the World Health Organization, about 4 million Sri Lankans still do not have water in their homes and a third of the rural population has no access to clean water or sanitation. As a result, every year, around a thousand Sri Lankans die from preventable water-borne diseases, according to World Vision.

Food security is another issue. Although a "crash" resettlement programme for war-affected families was carried out, many households remain in a persistent state of food insecurity long after their return to their original homelands. Due to logistical and financial barriers, a lack of access to diverse and healthy diets persists. The economic environment is not conducive to sustainable livelihoods given the need for large-scale infra-structure rehabilitation, land ownership issues and a lack of capital.

On environmental issues, as a developing island nation subject to tropical climate patterns, Sri Lanka is highly vulnerable to climate change impacts (Sri Lankan Ministry of Environment and Natural Resources, 2007). Extreme weather events, such as high intensity rainfall followed by flash floods and landslides and extended dry periods resulting in water scarcity, are becoming common.

The country's mean temperature is expected to rise by 1.2–1.6°C by 2050. The rainfall patterns also appear to have changed, with more rain in the mountainous, south-western wet zone and even less in the dry zone that only gets about 1,200–1,900 mm of annual rainfall versus 2,500 mm in wider-spread wet zone. With rainfall and climatic changes difficult to predict, adaptation becomes more challenging.

The destruction of crops by floods after severe droughts, especially over the past five years, exemplifies these changes. The nation's main crops – including rice, coconut and tea – are susceptible to rainfall and temper-ature. Hence, agricultural production will be severely affected by these changes.

Trends

According to an USAIDSri Lanka study in 2012, Sri Lankan companies spent LKR4 billion ($31 million) in CSR activities in 2012 (CSR Lanka, 2013). This has been spent by less than 50 companies. This is a trend that needs to be documented.

Sectors such as agriculture, aviation and apparel provide good examples of a growing trend towards adopting more sustainable activities and growing sustainable enterprises. For instance, to widen options for school dropouts, while building business sustainability, companies such as

Brandix and Sri Lankan Airlines have established industry-specific specialized education programmes.

A 2012 ILO survey named seven Sri Lankan companies – Hatton National Bank, Seylan Bank, Heritance Kandalama, part of the Aitken Spence group, Cinnamon Lodge hotel of the John Keells group, CKT Apparels, Mas Active (Pvt) Ltd and Halgolle Estate of Kelani Valley Plantations – for good practices in providing "green" jobs that ensure decent work for employees and environmental sustainability (LBO, 2012). The results reveal which Sri Lankan businesses are leading the way in transforming the country's economy with sustainable, low-carbon workplaces that provide decent work for people (EFC, 2012).

Government policies

The Central Environment Authority, Sustainable Energy Authority and several other national authorities have been created by statute and have been working for a few decades (Sri Lankan Ministry of Environment and Natural Resources, 2007). These provide policy frameworks and operational processes that mandate standards for all enterprises.

The fisheries development policy aims to leverage the country's fisheries and aquatic resources in a sustainable manner, while conserving the coastal environment. Key components include: development of deep-sea fisheries, freshwater fisheries and aquaculture, and minimizing post-harvest losses.

The Mahinda Chinthana policy framework indicates that the electricity sector's development will be focused on the sustainable development of energy resources, conversion facilities and delivery systems to improve the accessibility of energy services and ensure delivery at a regionally competitive price (Sri Lankan Department of National Planning, 2010).

The Sri Lanka Sustainable Energy Authority unveiled the 100% Renewable Energy Plan of Sri Lanka at the Asia Clean Energy Forum 2015 hosted by the Asian Development Bank (ADB), in Manila, Philippines.

Case studies

Brandix Lanka

Water is a core element of the clothing industry. To ensure the industry's responsibility and sustainability, Brandix Lanka initiated water-focused projects via its own Bindu Foundation. Registered in 2012, its flagship education programme trains women-led community organizations on water resource management. This programme addresses the critical need for capacity building at the community level especially to prepare for predicted climate change patterns which have drastic impacts on the water sector. Since inception, this programme has empowered over 500 such communities and a pilot activity in climate smart agriculture is also under way.

Hayleys Agriculture

Hayleys Agriculture Holdings practises an out-grower programme, which supports the livelihoods of about 10,000 farmers. The programme covers ten climatically diverse districts and includes fruits and locally novel crop-types such as gherkins, jalapeno peppers and Spanish peppers.

Using this approach, Hayleys has lower fixed overheads for its company-owned farms, yet is able to maintain continuous supplies throughout the year given the cultivation in different climatic zones. It is also able to meet orders more quickly by extending its indirect cultivation capacity.

The farming community meanwhile has security given the buy-back agreement they sign with the company. This programme also helps them introduce new seed varieties, apply organic fertilizer and compost and minimize pesticide usage with integrated pest management practices. It also introduced the safe use of low-toxin, eco-friendly crop protection products to reduce environmental pollution. Furthermore, the programme trains farmers on the latest agricultural developments and has successfully helped nurture farmer-entrepreneurs.

Kiruwanaganga Tea Estate

The Kiruwanaganga Tea Estate became Rainforest Alliance-certified in 2011, implementing an integrated sustainability programme. Its estates include a 41.5 ha protected high biodiversity area. These biodiversity blocks and wildlife habitats are identified on maps and protected with a

5 m chemical-free buffer zone and clear warning sign boards in community languages.

It has also converted its factories' tea driers from fossil fuel-based to wood-based renewable energy. Planting fuelwood is thus a continuous process at Kiruwanaganga's estates: over 400 ha were planted from 2007 to 2014.

This initiative alone reduced greenhouse gas emissions by over 3,000 tonnes CO_2 per annum. The carbon footprint in all estates is now measured and monitored to reduce carbon emissions annually.

The company also received the Presidential Award for the highest rate of replanting among all regional plantation companies from 2006 to 2011. It invested Rs. 2 billion in replanting tea from 1993 to 2013, which has now increased the vegetatively propagated (VP) tea percentage of the company to 65%.

Sadaharitha Plantations

Sadaharitha Plantations creates and manages forest plantations such as sandalwood, teak and Agarwood to generate opportunities for local and foreign investors. Once the expert team confirms a plot of land is suitable for cultivating a particular species, the plots are open for public investment. In addition to buying back the timber when the trees matured, Sadaharitha takes care of all maintenance during this time as well. Sadaharitha contributes to the environment to reduce the greenhouse emissions in the island, it also has the investment plan. Sadaharitha has planted about 600,000 of various plants such as teak, Mahogany Sandlewood and Agarwood across the island, which absorbed approximately 16,000 metric tonnes of carbon within the year 2014.

Further resources

Central Environmental Authority (CEA) – CEA was established in August 1981, under the provision of the National Environmental Act No.47. The Ministry of Environment was established in December 2001 with the overall responsibility for CEA affairs. Its objective is to integrate environmental considerations into the development process of the country.

CSR Sri Lanka – Established in 2013 to support responsible and sustainable enterprises, CSR Sri Lanka is providing expert knowledge and training on CSR best practice as a path to strategic transformation. With a growing membership, it currently has 35 member companies.

UN Global Compact Sri Lanka – Formed in April 2011, UNGC Sri Lanka consists of a Board and Steering Committee with the vision to drive corporate sustainability with global credibility – helping to position Sri Lankan businesses committed to embedding UN Global Compact principles on a global platform.

References

Central Bank of Sri Lanka (2013). Economic and Social Statistics of Sri Lanka 2013. Colombo: Statistics Department Central Bank of Sri Lanka.

CSR Lanka (2013). CSR in Sri Lanka – Key Findings. Colombo: CSR Lanka.

EFC (Employers' Federation of Ceylon) (2012). Going Green. 9 June 2012.

LBO (2012). Sri Lanka 'green' companies named by ILO. Lanka Business Online. 9 June 2012.

Sri Lankan Department of National Planning (2010). Mahinda Chinthana Vision for the Future. Colombo: Ministry of Finance and Planning.

Sri Lankan Ministry of Environment and Natural Resources (2007). Sri Lanka Strategy for Sustainable Development. Colombo: Ministry of Environment and Natural Resources.

20
Thailand

Ryan Young
Director of Applied Learning, Leder School of Business, Canada

Tatsanee Setboonsarng
Board Member and Executive Director, NawaChiOne Foundation, Thailand

National context

Frequently referred to as the "Land of Smiles", Thailand is well known as a tourist destination along the Malay Peninsula. But besides its beaches, Thailand is a diverse country both in geography and population. Its 64 million inhabitants are primarily ethnic Thai, but there are significant minority groups including Thai-Chinese, Malay and hill-tribe groups (Setboonsarng, 2010).

Thailand is a constitutional democracy with a parliamentary system where the leader of the largest party normally becomes the Prime Minister. Thailand's usually peaceful society has been marred by ten military *coups d'état* since 1932 (the last in 2006) and bouts of political protest activity in recent years.

Thailand's figurehead King Bhumibol Adulyadej is the world's longest-reigning monarch and is regarded as a stable presence in Thai society, providing a solid political foundation for the country. The civil service has also remained a steady force throughout the country's history. Thailand's free-enterprise market is well developed and diverse. Key industries include tourism, agriculture, tobacco, textiles and light manufacturing.

Priority issues

Once considered the fastest growing economy in Asia, recent statistics show that Thailand's political crisis has significantly slowed growth. Both tourism and export levels have declined in recent years and despite the government's attempt to bring stability through a snap election in early 2014, there appears to be no end in sight for the political unrest. Some governmental agencies, including those responsible for economic planning, have been closed since late 2013 due to protests. Once the political crisis has been resolved, however, it is likely that things will return to normal as the economy remains relatively strong.

Additionally, regional issues remain. The mainly Muslim regions in Thailand's southern provinces occasionally erupt in violence due to differences in religious views and separatist tendencies. Illegal Burmese immigrants frequently cross the border in the north causing social and economic challenges. During the past decade, the Thai government has spent considerable resources addressing these issues. Massive loan schemes have been created and universal health coverage now exists. Both loan and health programmes have been widely popular among the country's rural poor.

Like other developing nations, Thailand faces environmental challenges on three fronts: water, land and air. Problems of untreated water and drought rank Thailand low among Asian countries in terms of available clean water per capita. Air pollution poses another serious issue. While factory and vehicle emissions are the primary causes of poor air quality in Bangkok, burning of agricultural waste is the primary culprit in the northern regions. In preparation for the new planting season, pollution levels in the north can be reach hazardous levels for multiple days.

Trends

Championed by the king, Thailand has adopted a philosophy of a "sufficiency economy" as a middle path for developing a balanced and sustainable way of life for the country. Adopted as national policy since 1998, the framework encourages Thais to develop self-supporting and self-sufficient models where growth occurs in moderation. While the programme was adopted and applied to many segments of Thai society, a strong emphasis was placed on the farming and agricultural sectors. One popular programme demonstrated how small-scale farmers could create self-sufficient farms by dividing a six-hectare parcel of land into three main sections for the production of rice, fish and one other cash crop. Numerous model farms are scattered throughout the country as teaching sites for farmers in the area.

Government policies

Championed by the King of Thailand, the Sufficiency Economy Philosophy has been embedded within the country's National Economic and Social Development Plans for many years (Siripunyawit, 2014). With the goals of self-reliance, resilience and living in moderation, this philosophy is very compatible with the sustainability movement and has been promoted as such. A 1997 amendment to Thailand's constitution further strengthened the participation of civil society and the promotion of social innovation, but it was not until 2010 that specific policies were implemented. At that time, the National Social Enterprise Committee (NSEC) and Thailand Social Enterprise Office (TSEO) were established through a decree from the Prime Minister's Office (Government of Thailand, 2012).

The TSEO is a centre for policy development and management of social enterprises. It is an independent governmental agency and a national focal point for promoting social innovation and social enterprise throughout Thailand. The NSEC, on the other hand, focuses more on government policy by studying, proposing and advising the Cabinet on policies or strategies to promote activities on social enterprises. The NSEC also develops legal frameworks and coordinates with other agencies for implementing programmes to enhance social enterprises activities.

The establishment of these two agencies is the first phase in the country's Social Enterprise Master Plan (2010–14). The Plan focuses on four main strategies with subcommittees responsible for each strategy:

1. **Awareness and knowledge promotion** – Promoting awareness of social enterprises through national Social Enterprise (SE) awards and SE business plan competitions, conferences, media, and degree and non-degree programmes on sustainable entrepreneurship

2. **Model development and capacity building** – Developing criteria, legal frameworks, impact scopes and supporting laws and regulations for SEs

3. **Access to capital and resources development** – Developing mechanisms, processes and tools to promote funds, investment, financial intermediation and financial market services for SEs

4. **Public and private partnership promotion** – Modifying procurement regulations of government agencies to support SEs

These effects have not only made Thailand one of the most sophisticated in terms of structure but has also boosted interest in the sector especially among younger generations. Currently, there are an estimated 116,000 social enterprises in the country

Case studies

Andaman Discoveries

Andaman Discoveries was founded after the tsunami in 2004 as a responsible tourism operator that seeks to empower local villagers through the tourism industry. Their award-winning programmes were developed in collaboration with the communities in which they work and use local resources to have a positive human, environmental and financial impact.

Doi Chaang Coffee

Doi Chaang coffee produces high-quality organic Arabica coffee that is exported around the world through a joint venture between a group of Canadians and hill-tribe communities in a remote area near the Golden Triangle. Its mission is to bring economic and environmental sustainability to the indigenous hill-tribe communities, employing a philosophy of going "beyond fair trade". In addition to its cultural and environmental sensitivity, Doi Chaang investors have gifted 50% of the company's ownership and profits to its farmers. The company is lauded globally and has been the recipient of numerous awards including being one of the "Top 10 Small & Medium Enterprises" showcased at the 2012 United Nations Conference on Sustainable Development.

Grassroots Innovation Network Co., Ltd (GIN)

The Grassroots Innovation Network is a social enterprise using innovations to support organic agriculture and the wellbeing of villagers. GIN develops pro-poor sustainable agriculture methods and technologies that allow farmers to increase their yield and live in a healthy environment. It creates networks of community-based learning centres that introduce and incubate organic farming practices and appropriate technologies within the community. Initially, GIN earned its income from selling organic farming related products (fertilizer, earthworms, drip irrigation) and farm produce, as well as low-cost appropriate tools (farming tools, pollution-free cook stoves), growing through a network-marketing strategy. In the first year of establishment, GIN was able to increase quarter acre land yields by over 400%. It is now a listed company that raises funds by selling shares in the business.

Mae Fah Luang Foundation – Doi Tung Development Project

The Mae Fah Luang Foundation (MFLF) was founded by the mother of the current Thai king to focus on "improving social and economic development, preserving the environment and supporting local art and culture". The Foundation initially mainly supported the wellbeing of hill-tribe communities in Thailand's north, but has subsequently expanded into many other areas of sustainable development. One of its signature projects is the Doi Tung Development Project (DTDP) that aims, over a 30-year period, to turn a 15,000-hectare area once known for slash-and-burn agriculture and opium cultivation into one that protects the land while providing economic benefits for its residents. The project has been regarded as a major success and has been replicated globally.

NawaChiOne

The NawaChiOne Knowledge Center for Sufficiency Economy (NCO-KCSE) is a research and grass-roots capacity-building entity, founded in 2011, that promotes sustainable and climate friendly projects. It is a member of the Sukhothai Thammathirat Open University's Center of Distance Learning for Sufficiency Economy. Through the support of the NawaChiOne Foundation (NCOF), NCO-KCSE has delivered training on organic farming to local community groups. It has also developed the NawaChiOne organic rice demonstration farm using Bio-Energetic farming methods, which attracts many visitors. The farm's signature crop is organic black rice. It has demonstrated that new organic farming methods can save labour and overhead costs when farmers do not have to purchase fertilizer and pesticides. The foundation is now working with other NGOs and government entities to help convince farmers to switch to growing organically. It is also improving the supply chain, such as working with the post office to ship organic produce from the farms directly to consumers in a timely manner.

Further resources

Sasin Centre for Sustainable Management (SCSM) – Located within the business school at Chulalongkorn University and combining the principles of sustainable development, corporate social responsibility and HM King Bhumibol's Sufficiency Economy Philosophy to improve research and teaching of practices that create social, environmental, and economic balance. The centre also hosts a Net Impact professional chapter.

Thailand Business Council for Sustainable Development (TBCSD) – Has 36 high-profile corporate members and promotes environmental awareness within the business sector. Working in partnership with the Thailand Environmental Institute, the TBCSD operates the Green Label programme, which certifies products that have relatively low environmental impacts in their category.

Thailand Environmental Institute (TEI) – Founded on the belief that partnerships are the most effective approach in achieving sustainable development and a better quality of life. The TEI works closely with the private sector, government, local communities, other civil society organizations, academia and international partners to formulate environmental directives and link policy with action to encourage meaningful environmental progress in Thailand.

References

Government of Thailand (2012). Social Enterprise Master Plan 2010–2014 [in Thai], 29 May 2012. Bangkok: Government of Thailand.

Setboonsarng, T. (2010). Microfinance industry report. Thailand Foundation for Development Cooperation.

Siripunyawit, S. (2014, 24 February). Ploughing profitably. *Bangkok Post*.

21
Vietnam

Christopher Fleming
Associate Professor, Department of Accounting, Finance and Economics, and Asia–Pacific Centre for Sustainable Enterprise, Griffith University, Australia

Matthew Manning
Senior Lecturer, Centre for Aboriginal Economic Policy Research, The Australian National University, Australia

Do Trung Nguyen
PhD Candidate, Department of Accounting, Finance and Economics, Griffith University, Australia

National context

Vietnam is located in South-East Asia and borders China, Laos and Cambodia. Vietnam has a population of approximately 89 million, made up of over 50 distinct ethnic groups, dominated by the Kinh group (86.2% of the population). Almost half of the Vietnamese population practise indigenous religions, which include worshipping local spirits, gods and mother goddesses. Other major religions include Buddhism (16.4%) and Christianity (8.2%) (Pew Research Center, 2012).

Vietnam is widely considered to be an economic development success story. The nation has transformed from one of the world's poorest to boasting one of the fastest growing economies, with lower middle-income status attained in 2010. This transformation has been driven by the policy of "Doi Moi", which saw Vietnam move from a centrally planned economy to a socialist-oriented market economy from the mid-1980s onward. In

2013, Vietnam's Gross Domestic Product (GDP) was $171.4 billion. This corresponds to a per capita figure of $1,910. GDP growth for 2013 was 4.3%, and the average growth rate from 2000 to 2013 was 5.2% per annum (World Bank, 2014).

According to the 2014 United Nations' Human Development Index, Vietnam ranked 121st out of 187 countries, with a score of 0.638. This places Vietnam in the "medium" human development category. Between 1980 and 2013, Vietnam's Human Development Index value increased 37.8%, from 0.463 to 0.638. This score is above the average of the "medium" human development countries (0.614) but below the average for East Asia and Pacific Countries (0.703). In terms of the Multidimensional Poverty Index, which identifies multiple deprivations in the same households in education, health and standard of living, 6.4% of the population lived in multi-dimensional poverty while an additional 8.7% were near multi-dimensional poverty (United Nations Development Programme, 2014a).

Priority issues

In spite of Vietnam's remarkable economic progress over the previous two decades, a number of challenges remain. Significant issues include poverty and environmental degradation. With regard to the former, according to the 2013 Millennium Development Goals National Report (Ministry of Planning and Investment, 2013), the poverty rate in Vietnam decreased from 58% in 1992 to 9.6% in 2012. This overall reduction in poverty, however, is not evenly distributed, with poverty persisting among ethnic minorities (half of whom remain below the poverty line) and rural populations (United Nations Development Programme, 2014b).

This inequality in poverty is also reflected in other domains of life. For example, in 2013 Vietnam's Inequality-adjusted Human Development Index score was 14.9% below its unadjusted score, with inequality in education particularly problematic (United Nations Development Programme, 2014a). As noted by the United Nations Development Programme (2013), creating a more equitable and prosperous society will depend on success in regulating economic growth in environmentally sustainable ways, improving governance and distributing wealth and social services more evenly across society.

A number of environmental pressures exist in Vietnam. These include deforestation and soil degradation resulting from logging activities and the widespread practice of slash-and-burn agriculture. Fish stocks are also threatened by water pollution and overfishing. Although Vietnam has an abundance of groundwater resources, there are some major concerns around the quality of these resources. Poorly maintained septic tanks, garbage dumping, industrial effluents, over-exploitation and the presence of arsenic in parts of Hanoi, Ho Chi Minh City and the Mekong River Delta threaten groundwater supplies (World Environment Partnership in Asia, 2014).

Trends

Very little information exists on the state and trends of sustainable enterprise in Vietnam. Some information, however, is available on progress made under Government initiatives designed to promote sustainable business practice. For example, the Promoting Energy Conservation in Small and Medium-sized Enterprises initiative is reported to have completed 543 projects on energy conservation and efficiency across four manufacturing industries (ceramics, brick, paper and textiles) and food processing. Financial and economic benefits directly gained by small and medium-sized enterprises have resulted in a 10–50% reduction in production costs and a 30% increase in productivity. Further, the initiative has reduced CO_2 emissions by almost a million tonnes and lowered energy costs for these enterprises by approximately 24%.

An initiative to promote cleaner production in industry was recently completed in 2011 having carried out cleaner production demonstrations in 61 enterprises. The objective was to improve the livelihoods of workers and residents living around industrial areas through the adoption of cleaner production methods. The initiative undertook activities to support the adoption of cleaner production methods in 63 provinces and cities across Vietnam. These activities include training workshops and conferences, assessments of cleaner production possibilities for industrial enterprises and the development of cleaner production action plans at provincial levels. To date, little research has been conducted on the effectiveness of this initiative (Ministry of Planning and Investment, 2012).

Similarly, the Vietnam Cleaner Production Centre (VNCPC) was established in 1998 to disseminate and promote the cleaner production concept. In 2013, VNCPC implemented several projects including GetGreen Vietnam. The objective of GetGreen Vietnam is to contribute to increasing sustainable consumption behaviours of Vietnamese consumers and to increase capacity of consumer organizations and government in convincing and supporting consumers in making the choice for more sustainable consumption behaviour (Vietnam Cleaner Production Centre, 2014).

Government policies

In 2004, the Government of Vietnam issued a Strategic Orientation for Sustainable Development policy (Vietnam Agenda 21) and established a National Sustainable Development Council. The country's eight principles for sustainable development are largely focused on expanding economic activity, suggesting that: humans are at the centre of sustainable development; economic development is considered the central task of the next development period; and protection and improvement of environment quality are an inseparable factor of the development process.

There are 19 priority areas within the Strategic Orientation for Sustainable Development, including: switching to environmentally friendly production and consumption models; implementing the "clean industrialization" process; and ensuring sustainable agricultural and rural development. More recently, Prime Minister Nguyen Tan Dung approved the 2011–20 Vietnam Sustainable Development Strategy (Ministry of Planning and Investment, 2012).

The Government has also initiated a number of polices aimed at promoting the efficient use of energy and natural resources, and on pollution control and prevention. Relevant policies include: the establishment of an Environmental Protection Fund in 2002; the 2005 National Plan on Environmental Pollution Control; the 2006 National Targeted Programme on Energy Efficiency; the 2006 Programme on Energy Saving; the 2007 Proposal on Bio-fuel Development; and the 2009 Strategy on Cleaner Production in Industry (Ministry of Planning and Investment, 2012).

Vietnam has had ongoing issues in regards to working conditions and the treatment of workers. Issues include a lack of freedom of association and collective bargaining, an insufficient minimum wage, long working hours and the use of contract labour (where workers are offered only temporary or seasonal employment) (Wilshaw *et al.*, 2013). In response, in May 2013, a new Labor Code was introduced. This Code aimed to improve the labour market and industrial relations in Vietnam. Key changes include: increasing the minimum salary level during probation from 70% to 85% of a full salary; adding an extra day to the Lunar New Year holiday, bringing the total number of public holidays in Vietnam to ten; and increasing maternity leave from four to six months (Lee and Svanberg, 2013).

Case studies

KOTO (Know One, Teach One)

KOTO was established in 1999 by Vietnamese-Australian Jimmy Pham. The purpose of the organization is to positively contribute to the lives of disadvantaged youth in Vietnam by providing them with hospitality industry-related vocational training as well as English-language lessons and life skills. The first cohort of students graduated in 2002. Since then KOTO has trained more than 400 young people, with 25–30 new students being admitted every six months.

KOTO has two arms: a charity arm (KOTO Foundation) and a commercial arm (KOTO Enterprise). Operating training centres in Hanoi and Saigon, the charity arm offers a two-year training programme certified by the Australian-based Box Hill Institute. The commercial arm reflects the organization's social enterprise business model and is a means to generate income that supports the operational costs of the charity arm in order to improve the KOTO Foundation's capacity to train more students.

KOTO Enterprise consists of restaurants, catering services, a bakery and a cooking class. The medium-term objective is to expand into a boutique hotel and a commercial hospitality training centre. The long-term objective is to create a self-sustaining system, where KOTO Foundation can largely rely on its own resources and become less dependent on external funding (currently 75% of the funding for KOTO Foundation is from external philanthropic sources). Recognizing that the organization is a pioneer in social enterprise in Vietnam, KOTO is committed to sharing its model with others (KOTO, 2012).

Mai Vietnamese Handicrafts

Founded in 1990, Mai Vietnamese Handicrafts is a non-profit organization that provides income generation and marketing services to Vietnamese artists. Established by two social workers concerned about the lives of street children and single mothers, Mai Vietnamese Handicrafts has become the primary marketing agent for Vietnamese artisans from neglected families and women.

The organization has set up a decentralized network of 21 producer groups operating mainly in the southern provinces. This network has over 1,000 artists, 70% of whom are women. Each producer group specializes in a range of products that they sell and deliver to the organization, who act as the trading agent negotiating with local and international clients.

All profits go towards improving the living and working conditions of the poorest women in Vietnam, who often live on the street with their children. These women, often referred to as "dust of life", are often destined for prostitution, drug addiction and gang affiliation. The aim of Mai Vietnamese Handicrafts is to protect these women. Partner organizations include the 10,000 Villages, the Mennonite Central Committee, the World Fair Trade Organization, and the Vietnamese Chamber of Commerce and Industry (Nguyen-Stevenin, 2011; Ponle Cara al Comercio Justo, 2014).

Medical Technology Transfer and Services (MTTS)

MTTS was established in 2004 as an American-Vietnamese joint venture located in Hanoi, in recognition of the growing demand for affordable medical equipment. MTTS' mission is to promote and deliver appropriate, sufficient and reliable medical services to newborns and their parents in developing countries by adapting proven Western technologies to local communities. MTTS provide custom-designed, low-cost equipment to hospitals in Vietnam. They also provide targeted training to medical personal to treat infants suffering from common newborn illnesses.

MTTS strives to be a forerunner in the regulated use of chemical substances and is working towards the elimination of all hazardous substances in its products. As a sustainable enterprise, MTTS is currently developing all of their medical equipment to be powered by solar sources and intends to keep as much production as possible in Vietnam in order to help their workers and suppliers move towards economic self-sufficiency and stability. Only critical components that cannot be made locally are imported. Further, MTTS promotes incentive programmes such as share options to allow their staff to become greater stakeholders in the organization. MTTS aims to strengthen linkages with local health authorities to assist them in integrating their technologies into the larger health system.

MTTS is a main partner of Breath of Life, an East Meets West Foundation programme that directly addresses infant mortality in South-East Asia. Their collective work reflects the belief that every person deserves access to clean water, proper medical treatment and education. As a result of the programme, 24-hour infant mortality rates have dropped from 30% to 10% (Medical Technology Transfer and Services, 2009).

Further resources

The Vietnam Business Forum – Established as a project of the Vietnam Consultative Group at a meeting between the Vietnamese Government and its donor partners in 1997, the Vietnam Business Forum is a structured and ongoing policy dialogue between the Vietnamese Government and the local and foreign business community. The objective of the Forum is to foster a favourable business environment that attracts private-sector investment and stimulates sustainable economic growth.

The Vietnam Business Council for Sustainable Development (VBCSD) – Established in December 2010, VBCSD is a member-driven organization that aims to encourage its members and the wider business community to participate and contribute to sustainable development. Official members include a number of large multinational companies such as Unilever, Standard Chartered and LG.

References

KOTO (2012). Know one, teach one. Hanoi.

Lee, M. & Svanberg, A. (2013). Vietnam's new Labor Code: key changes for employers. *Tilleke & Gibbons*, 4, 1-2.

Medical Technology Transfer and Services (2009). Who we are. Hanoi: Medical Transfer and Services.

Ministry of Planning and Investment (2012). Vietnam: Some good sustainable development practices. Hanoi: Ministry of Planning and Investment.

Ministry of Planning and Investment (2013). Millennium Development Goals full report 2013: Vietnam. Hanoi: Ministry of Planning and Investment.

Nguyen-Stevenin, Q. (2011). Mai Vietnamese handicrafts: crafting a brighter tomorrow for disadvantaged women and minorities in Vietnam. New York: United Nations Development Programme.

Pew Research Center (2012). Religious composition by country. Washington, DC: Pew Research Center.

Ponle Cara al Comercio Justo (2014). Put a face on fair trade: Mai Vietnamese handicraft. Madrid: Ponle Cara al Comercio Justo.

United Nations Development Programme (2013). About Vietnam. New York: UNDP.

United Nations Development Programme (2014a). Explanatory note on the 2014 Human Development Report composite indices: Vietnam. New York: UNDP.

United Nations Development Programme (2014b). UNDP administrator trip to Vietnam to focus on issues facing Vietnam as middle-income country. New York: UNDP.

Vietnam Cleaner Production Centre (2014). Annual report 2013. Hanoi: Vietnam Cleaner Production Centre.

Wilshaw, R., Unger, L., Chi, D. & Thuy, P. (2013). Labour rights in Unilever's Supply chain: from compliance towards good practice. *An Oxfam study of labour issues in Unilever's Vietnam operations and supply chain*. Oxford: Oxfam.

World Bank (2014). Data: Vietnam. Washington, DC: World Bank.

World Environment Partnership in Asia (2014). State of water environmental issues: Vietnam. Yokosuka: World Environment Partnership in Asia.

About the editor

Wayne Visser, PhD, is Director of the think-tank and media company, Kaleidoscope Futures, and describes himself as a professional idea-monger, storyteller and meme-weaver. His work as a strategy analyst, sustainability adviser, CSR expert, futurist and professional speaker has taken him to over 70 countries in the past 20 years to work with over 130 clients, ranging from companies such as Coca-Cola, Dell, DHL and HSBC to international organizations  such as the United Nations Environment Programme (UNEP), the World Bank and Worldwide Fund for Nature (WWF).

Wayne is a prolific writer and global lecturer, believing that we learn the best by constantly challenging ourselves to research, teach and write. He is the author of 24 books – including *Sustainable Frontiers: Unlocking Change Through Business, Leadership and Innovation* – and a guest columnist for *The Guardian* newspaper. He holds an academic Chair in Sustainable Business at the Gordon Institute of Business Science in South Africa and is a Senior Associate and Masters Tutor at Cambridge University's Institute for Sustainability Leadership.

Wayne sees his mission as helping to bring about transformative thinking and action in business and society. This begins, he says, with "letting go an industrial system that has served us well, but is no longer fit for purpose; old styles of leadership and outdated models of business; high-impact life-styles and selfish values; cherished ideologies that are causing destruction; and beliefs about ways to tackle problems that are failing to resolve crises".

Reaching sustainable frontiers, therefore, "must begin with changing our collective minds – and only then will we change our collective behaviour".

Wayne has been recognized as one of the world's top 48 "thriveability" leaders (2015), a top 100 influencer on Twitter in CSR and sustainable business (2014), a top 100 thought-leader in trustworthy business (2013) and a top 100 global sustainability leader (2012). He is also the recipient of the Global CSR Excellence and Leadership Award (2013), the Emerald Literati Outstanding Author Contribution Award (2011) and the Outstanding Teacher Award of the Warwick MBA (2010/11 and 2011/12).

In 2009, Wayne founded CSR International, after obtaining a PhD in corporate social responsibility in the UK and having previously served as Director of Sustainability Services for KPMG and Strategy Analyst for Capgemini in South Africa. His other qualifications include an MSc in Human Ecology (Edinburgh University, UK) and a Bachelor of Business Science with Honours in Marketing (Cape Town University, South Africa). In 2015, Wayne seeded the global Walk for Trees movement. He lives in Cambridge and enjoys art, nature, writing poetry and learning about new countries and cultures.

A full biography and much of his writing and art is on www.waynevisser.com.

About the contributors

Chandula Abeywickrema [contributor for **Sri Lanka**] is Chairman of Banking with the Poor Network, Asia's largest microfinance network. Chandula serves as the Managing Director/CEO of CCC Solutions, a fully owned subsidiary company of Sri Lanka's largest business chamber, the Ceylon Chamber of Commerce. He is an accomplished commercial banker with lead expertise, and experience in retail and development banking spanning over 30 years at Hatton National Bank. Chandula is the Chairman of the board of CSR Sri Lanka, the national apex body for corporate and sustainable responsibility in Sri Lanka. He serves on boards of a number of Sri Lankan and international financial institutions.

Azlan Amran [contributor for **Malaysia**] is an Associate Professor at the Graduate School of Business, Universiti Sains Malaysia (USM). At present, he holds the position of Deputy Dean (Academic and Student Affairs) at the Graduate School of Business. He is a member of the editorial board for several international journals. At the national level, he is a Technical Committee member for ISO 26000 (Social Responsibility).

Azhar Baisakalova, PhD [contributor for **Kazakhstan**] is an Assistant Professor in Public Policy and Management at the Department of Public Administration at the KIMEP University, in Almaty, Kazakhstan. Her teaching and research interests are in the fields of public administration and management, public policy and corporate social responsibility, tourism and management, research methods and statistics, and gender and public policy. She combines her academic activities with consultancy in corporate social responsibility and sustainable development to public, non-governmental and international organizations. Dr Baisakalova has published articles and conference papers in various international journals and conference proceedings.

Khadeeja Balkhi [contributor for **Maldives** and **Sri Lanka**] is a multiple award-winning journalist. She began practising journalism in South Carolina and then Jeddah, with *The Saudi Gazette*. She has published over 200 articles, several confidential reports and strategies. She founded a Sustainability Consultancy in 2004 and the specialized journal and platform "tbl: triple-bottom-line". She was Chairman of the CSR Standing Committee for the Federation of Pakistan Chambers of Commerce and Industry (FPCCI). She trains diverse groups, works with academia and chairs award juries. Having studied International Business, Creative Writing and Chemistry in the USA, she is currently enjoying her PhD learning.

Theresa Bauer, PhD [contributor for **Malaysia**] is Professor of International Management and Marketing at SRH FernHochschule Riedlingen. She has work experience as a lecturer at Raffles University Iskandar (Johor Bahru, Malaysia) and as a public relations manager in Germany. She received her PhD from Humboldt-University Berlin, Germany, as well as degrees in History and Multimedia from Karlsruhe University, Germany, and degrees in Economics and Business Administration from Hagen University, Germany. Her current research focuses on CSR, Responsible Lobbying and CSR Communication.

Lorne Butt, PhD [contributor for **Papua New Guinea**] is the Sustainability Coordinator at TAFE NSW Western Institute. Lorne trained as a biologist before joining the higher education sector. With a background in quality management, strategic planning and corporate governance, Lorne now specializes in sustainability practice, governance, education and research. Lorne is an Associate Fellow of the Australian Institute of Management, and a member of the British and Australia/New Zealand academies of management, the Australian Institute of Company Directors, and the Australian Association of Environmental Educators. Lorne is also a member of the Advisory Board for the Institute for Land, Water and Society at Charles Sturt University.

Markus Dietrich [contributor for the **Philippines**] is the founder of ASEI Inc., an inclusive business and renewable energy consulting, research and project development firm in the Philippines, and co-founder of Hilltribe Organics, a social enterprise lifting hill-tribe communities in northern

Thailand out of poverty. His engagements with Asian Development Bank, World Bank, UNDP, GIZ and corporate clients have resulted in enabling policies and scalable business models advancing his vision of inclusive growth powered by renewable energy. He contributed to various publications; the latest is *Base of the Pyramid 3.0*, edited by Stuart Hart.

Christopher Fleming, PhD [contributor for **New Zealand** and **Vietnam**] is an Associate Professor at Griffith Business School and the Director of the Master of Business Administration (MBA) programme. Christopher is also a founding member of the Griffith Centre for Sustainable Enterprise. Prior to joining Griffith University, Christopher worked as a Senior Consultant for Marsden Jacob Associates and as a Senior Advisor within the Sustainable Development Policy Group of the New Zealand Ministry for the Environment. Christopher holds a Bachelor of Arts (Economics) from the University of Otago, a Master of Applied Economics with first class honours from Massey University and a PhD (Economics) from the University of Queensland.

Akash Ghai [contributor for **Cambodia** and **Pakistan**] has detailed experience in assessing the impact of business support operations, corporate governance and strategic planning on programme delivery and organizational development of NGOs. Akash places emphasis on building a strong organizational structure so that NGOs can deliver quality programmes that help their beneficiaries while maintaining financial sustainability. He has extensive International Relations experience and has led a number of global projects for the Commonwealth. Akash is currently based in New York City and has worked on numerous International and Social Development projects, ranging from sanitation in Madagascar to charitable direction for a natural health organization.

Juniati Gunawan, PhD [contributor for **Indonesia**] is Director of Trisakti Sustainability Center (TSC), Trisakti University. She graduated with a PhD in Corporate Social Reporting from Edith Cowan University, Western Australia and specializes in sustainability reporting. She is a senior lecturer at Trisakti University, Jakarta, a guest lecturer and speaker in national and overseas education institutions, a member of international journal editorial boards in social and environmental accounting, and social responsibility under Ebsco, Emerald and Cabell's Publishing. As a practitioner, she serves on a number of organizations from various industries and on an expert committee for corporate social responsibility awards events in Indonesia.

Md Nazmul Hasan [contributor for **Bangladesh**] is a doctoral researcher and graduate teaching assistant at Royal Holloway, University of London. He is also the recipient of the prestigious "Dean's Scholar in Management" award. He has qualifications in International Business Economics (MSc, with distinction) and Management Research (ESRC-recognized MRes, with distinction) from Dundee and Stirling. Hasan is passionate about sustainable development, be it at the national, regional or global level, and his broad research interests are also in this area. He is particularly interested in sustainability in global value chains and environmental reform in developing economies

Colin Higgins, PhD [contributor for **Australia**] is Senior Lecturer in the Deakin Business School where he teaches sustainability, strategy and CSR. He is Deputy Director of Deakin's Centre for Sustainable and Responsible Organizations (CSaRO). His research focuses on how business organizations are influenced by, but also shape, the broader sustainability agenda.

Verrome Hutchinson [contributor for the **Philippines**] is a specialist in the fields of entrepreneurship and small and medium enterprise development with a focus on Inclusive Business and Corporate Social Responsibility (CSR). She has gained experience as an entrepreneur, in private-sector companies and an international organization supporting public-sector programmes for entrepreneurs. Ms Hutchinson holds a MSc from the University of London in Entrepreneurship.

Md Shafiqul Islam [contributor for **Bangladesh**] is an Assistant Professor at the Centre for Sustainable Development (CSD), University of Liberal Arts Bangladesh. At present he is doing a PhD at the Institute of Disaster Management and Vulnerability Studies, University of Dhaka, Bangladesh. He has done extensive research in the field of nature conservation, agricultural production, sector assessment and bio-intensive gardening. His research interests include natural resource management, landscape and agro-forestry, climate change adaptation, drought and integrated water management, organic farming, biodiversity and nature conservation, sustainable city, grass-roots economic development, green business, indigenous knowledge, sustainable development, sustainable livelihoods and development planning.

Muneezay Jaffery [contributor for **Cambodia** and **Pakistan**] is the operations manager at a London-based charity, Green Shoots Foundation, working on healthcare agriculture and education projects in Asia. She has more than five years' work experience in the non-profit sector doing strategic planning, organizational assessment and project monitoring and evaluation for small and start-up NGOs, non-profits and social enterprises. She is the Assistant Editor and contributor for the book *Sustainable [R]evolutions* (2014) and other consulting projects have included dialogue sessions with non-profits and an ESG framework for a microfinance fund manager. Muneezay trained as a Corporate Social Responsibility analyst at Ernst & Young between 2007 and 2009.

Lauren James [contributor for **Australia**] is Commercialisation and Vendor Assurance Manager for Fonterra Brands. She has sustainability consulting experience across multiple industries including FMCG, financial services, agriculture, government and NGOs in Australasia, Europe, USA and Latin America. Some of the companies and clients she has worked for include PWC, UK; Pernod Ricard; Bank of New Zealand (NAB Group); SPC Ardmona and Department of Health, Victoria; Republic of Everyone, Australia; Chime, Italy. She is currently completing sustainability advisory work for Fonterra, the global dairy giant.

Angela Joo-Hyun Kang [contributor for **South Korea**] is Founder and Executive President of Global Competitiveness Empowerment Forum (GCEF) based in Seoul, South Korea. Ms Kang is currently Regulation Reform Committee Member of the Ministry of Industry, Trade, and Energy, Advisor of Korea Social Enterprise Promotion Agency, and Steering Committee Member of UN Global Compact Network Korea. She was Advisor of Presidential Council of Nation Branding and Evaluation Member of leadership and responsible practices of state-owned enterprises appointed by the Ministry of Strategy and Finance. She holds a mid-career Master's degree of Public Administration from Harvard Kennedy School where she was also Mason Fellow and Asia Program Fellow.

Kazunori Kobayashi [contributor for **Japan**] graduated from University of California, Berkeley, and since 1999 has been locally and internationally engaged in planning and implementing projects and writings dedicated to sustainability. Since 2005, he has served as the President of EcoNetworks, a team of specialists in languages, the environment, business, culture and other diverse fields. The team shares the same vision of creating sustainable societies and its network spans more than 100 countries worldwide. He is also a lecturer at the University of Tokyo, and currently writing his PhD thesis on human sustainability and employee wellbeing at Massey University, New Zealand.

Aparna Mahajan, MBA [contributor for **Central, East and South Asia and India**] is a management and development practitioner. She has been an International Technical Expert with UNDP Somalia, Kenya; Country Specialist and Consultant in Private Sector/CSR with UNV and UNDP, India; Advisor, Corporate Communications, TERI, India; and Programs Specialist with Dubai Chamber of Commerce and Industry, UAE. Earlier, she worked on specialized leadership assignments with the Federation of Indian Chambers of Commerce and Industry, IIT Delhi, and Nestlé India Ltd. Aparna has several publications to her credit in diverse fields, including being an Expert Contributor for *The World Guide to CSR* (2010) by CSR International, UK and authoring India Country Report on Enhancing Business-Community Relations (2004) by United Nations Volunteers Hqrs, Germany. Currently, Aparna is Director, Resource Mobilization and Partnerships at S M Sehgal Foundation, India.

Arunima Malik [contributor for **Norfolk Island**] is a researcher at ISA, School of Physics at the University of Sydney. Her research area is hybrid life-cycle assessment and triple-bottom-line footprinting. She is interested in undertaking sustainability analysis of renewable energy technologies. In particular, Arunima has analysed the social effects of introducing a new biofuels industry in Australia, and the triple-bottom-line analysis of biofuel production using forestry and algae feedstocks. She holds a Bachelor of Science (Molecular Biology and Genetics) with Honours in Plant Cell Biology and Masters of Teaching. Prior to joining ISA, Arunima was a molecular biologist extracting and analysing DNA samples from terrestrial plants.

Matthew Manning, PhD [contributor for **New Zealand** and **Vietnam**] is an economist in the Centre for Aboriginal Economic Policy Research, the Australian National University. Matthew applies economic and econometric methods for investigating and evaluating social interventions/programmes (e.g. cost–benefit analysis and time-series modelling); moreover, to shape appropriate policy around current social issues. Matthew also uses operations research methods (e.g. multi-criteria analysis) to investigate complex problems and develop mathematically sound solutions to those problems. Matthew holds a Bachelor of Commerce (Economics), a Master of Arts with honours and a PhD in Economics.

Do Trung Nguyen [contributor for **Vietnam**] is a PhD candidate in Economics at Griffith University. Prior to joining the PhD programme, Trung spent nine years as a transportation infrastructure specialist.

His research interests include social and economic programme evaluation, regulatory impact assessment, cost–benefit analysis in infrastructure economics and transport economics. Trung holds a Bachelor of International Trade (Economics), a Master of Investment Economics from the National Economics University of Vietnam.

Yanuar Nugroho, PhD [contributor for **Indonesia**] is a Research Fellow at Manchester Business School and Deputy Chief of Staff for the Analysis and Oversight of Priority Programme at the Executive Office of the President of the Republic of Indonesia. He is a Research Fellow in Innovation and Social Change with the Manchester Business School (MBS) at the Institute of Innovation Research (MIOIR). Since October 2012, he has been seconded to the Indonesian Government as a director and special adviser to the Minister Head of the Indonesian President's Delivery Unit for Development Monitoring and Oversight (UKP4) and since March 2014 assumes his current role at the Executive Office of the President. His research interests and publications cover innovations in the third sector, development and sustainability, media and social change, and knowledge dynamics.

Swe Sett Kyu Pe [contributor for **Myanmar**] is currently completing a Masters of Engineering programme specializing in Energy Systems at Griffith University. Previously he worked as an electrical engineer in an Australian engineering firm that deals with high voltage electrical machines. He was graduated with a Bachelor of Engineering (Electrical) degree from University of Queensland in 2010. He also obtained a Diploma in Electronics, Computer and Communication Engineering from Singapore Polytechnic in 2003. After graduating from Singapore Polytechnic, he worked in Singapore as an associate engineer for nearly five years. He is originally from Myanmar and currently resides in Brisbane, Australia.

Semerdanta Pusaka, DBA [contributor for **Indonesia**] is Director of Aicón Strategic Sustainability Management, Director of Sandikta College of Administrative Sciences, and one of founders of the International Society of Sustainability Professionals (ISSP), Indonesia. He graduated with a DBA from De La Salle University, Manila, Philippines. With his expertise in accounting, finance, business administration, corporate communications and sustainability, he serves NGOs, MNCs and large national companies in various sectors, such as education, mining, fertilizers, food and beverages, pulp and paper and banking. He also co-founded the International Society of Sustainability Professionals (ISSP), Indonesia. His research interests are sustainable business, urban metabolism, SME development and change management.

Denise Quintal [contributor for **Norfolk Island**] is an Executive Director of EcoNorfolk Foundation Inc Limited and believes that decisions made by the Foundation can only be clearly defined by scientific evidence. She is committed to the science of sustainability and drives the Foundation with this continued aim and objective. EcoNorfolk has been active since 2003 by highlighting issues such as waste and the environmental impact of island enterprises, and has established protocols for education and funding purposes. By developing international partnerships the Foundation now showcases these successful programmes to overseas groups and research students. Denise writes papers, convenes conferences and facilitates motivational think-tanks.

Tapan Sarker, PhD [contributor for **Myanmar** and **Papua New Guinea**] is the Discipline Leader of Sustainable Enterprise at Griffith Business School. He is a former World Bank scholar. Previously he worked as a research fellow at the Centre for Social Responsibility in Mining of the University of Queensland and as a researcher in the Japanese programme of Leadership for Environment and Development. Tapan holds a PhD in sustainable business management from the Australian National University. He is a member of the Australia New Zealand Academy of Management, the Academy of International Business, and the British Academy of Management. He is an editorial board member of the Journal of Corporate Citizenship.

Tatsanee Setboonsarng [contributor for **Thailand**] is the Executive Director for NawaChiOne Foundation, a grass-roots entity in Thailand that promotes sustainable development solutions, consistent with the Sufficiency Economy Philosophy (SEP). She has extensive experience working in both private multinational companies and international organizations. Tatsanee is a frequent guest lecturer at Kasetsart University, Bangkok, Thailand. In addition, she has received accreditation from the Microfinance Training-of-Trainers programme through the World Bank. Tatsanee holds two MA degrees from the University of Oregon, in International Studies and in Public Affairs.

Jimmy Tanaya, PhD [contributor for **Indonesia**] is Research Director at the Centre for Innovation Policy and Governance (CIPG) and CEO of Aicón Strategic Sustainability Management. He completed his jointly administered doctoral training at the Sustainable Consumption Institute and Manchester Business School, University of Manchester. His research interests are the role of business in society, business models, innovation and strategic CSR. He co-founded and runs CIPG, a research-based advocacy group, and Aicón Strategic Sustainability Management. He has been advising on a number of CSR strategic planning projects among companies in Indonesia. He also co-founded and is a member of the International Society of Sustainability Professionals (ISSP), Indonesia.

Thomas Thomas [contributor for **Singapore**] is CEO of the ASEAN CSR Network, a network of Corporate Social Responsibility networks in ASEAN. Thomas is a member of the UN Economic and Social Commission for Asia Pacific's Business Advisory Council; the lead of the ASEAN Intergovernmental Commission on Human Rights study team on CSR in ASEAN and an Honorary Professor of CSR with the Nottingham University Business School, UK. Thomas was the founding Executive Director of the Singapore Compact for CSR, co-chair of National Tripartite Initiative for CSR, Focal Point for UN Global Compact and in developing ISO 26000 guidance standard on social responsibility.

Kaumadee Weeraratne [contributor for **Sri Lanka**] has a BA (Hons.) Degree in Business Administration from Staffordshire University, UK, and is an Associate Member of Charted Institute of Marketing. She joined Hayleys plc in 2008. The fields she explored within this period of six years include international marketing, strategic business development, corporate communications and sustainability. She currently serves as Head of Operations for CSR Sri Lanka.

Jeremy B. Williams, PhD [contributor for **South-East Asia and Oceania**) is an ecological economist with global experience in universities and at a senior executive level in the private sector. He has taught courses in sustainable development, sustainable enterprise and environmental management (online and on campus), and has worked with a number of companies around the world to improve their understanding of sustainability issues through executive education. Jeremy is also an education futurist, and widely acknowledged as a pioneer in technology enhanced learning. His latest project is a start-up sustainable enterprise, of which he is co-founder, Green School for Girls, which was launched in 2015.

Karina Yadav [contributor for **India**] is a corporate sustainability and responsibility (CSR) professional focusing on sustainability agendas in

Asia and Europe. Her main research area comprises of the state of CSR in India, including the role of the government to institutionalize CSR. She has co-authored The CSR International Research Compendium. Besides her research interest, Karina is managing India Business & Biodiversity Initiative (IBBI), hosted by the Confederation of Indian Industry (CII). Karina is Founder of an advisory firm CSRway. Prior to this, she has served as Managing Director of the think-tank CSR International. She holds MSc in CSR from Nottingham University Business School's (UK) International Centre for Corporate Social Responsibility (ICCSR).

Ryan Young [contributor for **Thailand**] is the Director of Applied Learning at the Leder School of Business (The King's University) in Edmonton, Canada. His current interests are in social entrepreneurship, microfinance, entre-preneurship and strategy. Ryan founded and managed one of Thailand's largest non-governmental microfinance institutions. He currently sits on several boards including a renewable energy cooperative and a large multi-national relief and development organization.

M. Rizvi Zaheed [contributor for **Sri Lanka**] is Managing Director of Hayleys Agriculture. Rizvi is also Director, Sri Lanka Institute of Nanotechnology (SLINTEC). He is Co-Chair, National Council on Biotechnology; Council Member, Sri Lanka Council for Agricultural Research Policy (CARP); Member, Main Committee, Ceylon Chamber of Commerce; Member, University Grants Commission Agriculture Advisory Committee; Member, Sri Lanka Export Development Board Advisory Committee on Food & Beverages; and Vice Chairman of CSR Sri Lanka. Rizvi has a BA (Hons.), and holds an MBA degree from the University of Colombo. He has presented at several global forums on agriculture, sustainability and management.

Shuyi Zhang, PhD [contributor for **China**] is a full-time professor in the School of Innovation and Entrepreneurship at Shanghai Finance University. He obtained his doctorate in Management Science and Engineering after an extensive career in business. His research interest focuses on tech-nology innovation, entrepreneurship and corporate social responsibility. Besides conducting research programme on sustainable enterprise, he has published more 50 academic papers nationally and internationally, including in *International Entrepreneurship and Management Journal* and *European Journal of International Management*.

Other volumes of the World Guide to Sustainable Enterprise

Volume 1 – Africa and the Middle East

Regional profiles

Middle East and North Africa

Sub-Saharan Africa

Country profiles

Angola

Botswana

Cameroon

Egypt

Eritrea

Ghana

Iran

Israel

Jordan

Kenya

Lebanon

Lesotho

Madagascar

Mauritius

Morocco

Namibia

Nigeria

Oman

Qatar

Rwanda

Saudi Arabia

Senegal

South Africa

South Sudan

Tanzania

Turkey

Uganda

United Arab Emirates

Volume 3 – Europe

Regional profiles
Eastern and southern Europe
Northern and western Europe

Country profiles
Armenia
Austria
Belarus
Bosnia and Herzegovina
Bulgaria
Croatia
Czech Republic
Denmark
Estonia
Finland
France
Georgia
Germany
Greece
Greenland
Hungary
Iceland
Italy
Latvia
Lithuania
Macedonia
Moldova
Montenegro
Netherlands
Norway
Poland
Portugal
Romania
Slovakia
Spain
Sweden
Switzerland
United Kingdom

Volume 4 – The Americas

Regional profiles
Northern and Central America
South America

Country profiles
Argentina
Brazil
Canada
Chile
Colombia
Costa Rica
Cuba
Dominica
Dominican Republic
Ecuador
Guatemala
Guyana
Haiti
Mexico
Panama
Suriname
Trinidad and Tobago
United States of America
Uruguay